Ace Attorney Investigations Collection

Latest Guide with Full Walkthrough | Large Size Edition | Colorful Pages | A Must Have to Master the Game

By

Amelia Anderson

Table of Contents

GAMEPLAY

Investigation Phase

In investigation phase, you can navigate around the surroundings. You can consult your partner if you currently have one, though it is usually not necessary to advance through the game. You can also **talk** to people and **examine** objects that are of interest. Examining certain objects will let you enter a close-up scene where you can examine the scene closer. Edgeworth will hint about whether you have already found all the clues you need in a close-up scene. If he says he feels like

he has all he needs from the scene, that means further investigation of the scene will be pointless.

There is no "move" feature in this game as you can go to different locations by walking to its entrance, which is indicated by a green arrow when you approach it.

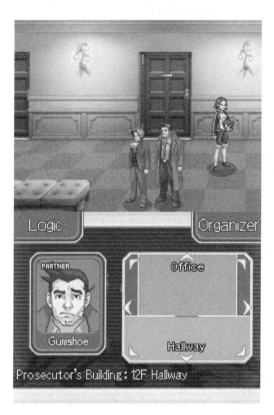

DEDUCTION

Sometimes, there will be a contradiction in a close-up scene or even a piece of evidence. You will be required to pinpoint the location of the contradiction on the scene. You must then **deduce** that spot and **present** the evidence that proves the contradiction.

Confrontation Mode

This mode happens between investigation modes. You will face your opponent in a battle of wits. It is similar to cross-examination in the old games. You can **press** for more information and **present** evidence when something in the testimony contradicts it. You will often need to press certain statements in order to get new statements that have a contradiction.

Organizer

The organizer holds all of your evidence and profiles on important characters, so it's a good idea to have a look through it from time to time. You can **examine** certain pieces of evidence, either to read a document, view a photo or physically examine the object. Some objects can be examined three-dimensionally, the angle of which can be tweaked using the touchscreen or the button controls.

Logic

The new feature in this game is Logic. As you investigate you will come across logic segments. You're required to join these segments to form a new segment or an entirely new piece of evidence.

Health Bar

There is a health bar like the previous games. If you present wrong evidence or connect logic segments unsuccessfully, your health bar will sustain damage. If your health bar is emptied, it is an instant game over. The health bar will be replenished halfway at the final investigation or confrontation of the chapter.

Saving

Saving can be done either by pressing start at any point during the game or at the end of a chapter. Saving halfway in a chapter will immediately make you exit the game, which you can continue anytime. Saving at the end of a chapter will instead advance you to the next chapter, unless it's the final chapter of a case, where it will just return you to the case-select screen. Saves act as checkpoints that you can return to after a game over, so if you're in a difficult portion of the game, make sure to save often.

Turnabout Bad Endings

If you played Ace Attorney Turnabout Episodes that has more than one ending, then perhaps you should suspend your disbelief because in all five episodes of this game, there's about seven bad endings each depending on when and where you're health bar empties out. Save and experiment where you've gone wrong unless you want to see the bad endings. But everyone wants a good ending so be careful and save often.

CONTROLS

Button	Action
⊹	Move Edgeworth
Ⓐ	• Examine objects • Talk to characters • Advance through dialogues/testimonies • Confirm selection
Ⓑ	• Hold to run • Go back through testimony statements • Cancel selection • Go back through menus • Hold to advance quickly through dialogues, where possible
Ⓧ	• Talk to your partner during investigations • Present evidence during testimonies • Connect logic • Deduce during examining of objects
	• Zoom in when using the 3D viewer
Ⓨ	• Hold to activate microphone where available • Zoom out when using the 3D viewer
Ⓛ	• Open Logic menu during investigations • Press during testimonies
Ⓡ	• Open Organizer • Switch between Evidence and Profiles
◯START	Save game

CHARACTERS

Miles Edgeworth

The character you control in this game, Edgeworth is a prosecutor who strives for the truth. He is very intelligent and has very intimidating tactics of interrogation. He tends to be a little of a perfectionist. Due to an incident in his childhood he has a deep fear of earthquakes and elevators.

Dick Gumshoe

Dick Gumshoe will help you in the cases of this game. He tends to be very dimwitted and forgetful. Phoenix Wright fans should be able to remember him.

Franziska von Karma

Franziska is the daughter of the feared Manfred von Karma. Like her father, she aims for one thing in her family's life, perfection. She is working with the Interpol on investigating about an international smuggling ring.

Kay Faraday

A peppy teenager who claims to be the Great Thief Yatagarasu. She met Edgeworth during a case seven years ago.

Shi-Long Lang

An Interpol agent from the Republic of Zheng Fa. He has a strong hatred for prosecutors and the courtroom. He looks after his men really well. Often quotes Lang Zi.

Shih-na

Shi-Long Lang's assistant. She keeps scrolls of Lang Zi quotes as well as information regarding the cases Lang is investigating.

Calisto Yew

The defense attorney for a trial seven years ago. She tends to break down into a fit of laughter from the mildest things, like Edgeworth's serious attitude.

Tyrell Badd

A seasoned detective who investigated the Yatagarasu. He is an acquaintance of Byrne Faraday and has worked with him in a lot of cases.

Yatagarasu

A mysterious thief that steals information of corrupt dealings and makes them public.

WALKTHROUGH

TURNABOUT VISITOR

Part 1-1 - Beginning

You walk towards your office, musing about the previous days and having been gone for a month since your last case. As you open your office door, you find that it is unlocked. You enter your office to find... a body. Suddenly, someone emerges behind you with a gun drawn. After a brief conversation, they shoot the framed jacket in the room and leave.

Sometime later, forensics officers have arrived at the scene. Suddenly, a detective bursts in. Anybody who has played an Ace Attorney game before will recognize him as Detective Dick Gumshoe! After a little conversation, you will wonder why the crime happened in your office, giving you the **Crime scene: My office** logic. Afterwards, Gumshoe will say that **The office key** was with him the whole time. You will be introduced to a new mechanic in this game called the logic system. Press L or the "Logic" icon with ✏ to enter Logic mode, where you must match two pieces of logic that have a connection.

However, if you make a wrong connection, your "truth meter" (the green health bar) will decrease, and if it empties, the truth will be lost forever (and the game is over). For now, there are only two pieces of logic. Connect **Crime scene: My office** with **The office key**. Congratulations! You have connected the first two pieces of logic in the game. You deduce that the murder in your office was no coincidence, but why did the killer pick here? **The killer's goal** is currently unclear.

Investigation

You can now freely walk around your office with ✚ or holding the map icon in the direction you wish to move (hold Ⓑ or the arrows around the map icon to run) and you can consult Gumshoe by pressing Ⓨ or the "Partner" icon. For now, **Examine** the **Revolver** that the murderer dropped by approaching it and pressing Ⓐ or the "Examine" icon. Gumshoe recognizes it as the same model used by the precinct.

Now, approach to the dead body and **examine** it. You will enter a subscreen that allows you a closer look at the crime scene. **Examine** the black object next to the body. It's a badge that identifies the body as Detective Buddy Faith; looks like the **Victim was a detective**. Now **examine** the body itself. The victim was fatally shot once through his abdomen. The body was found at 2:05 AM by you. The **Crime Scene Notes** will be stored in the Organizer, which you can refer to it at any time by pressing R or the "Organizer" icon to check the evidence you've collected, along with profiles of people you've met thus far. **Examine** the toppled files at the top of the screen. Looks like **Signs of a struggle**.

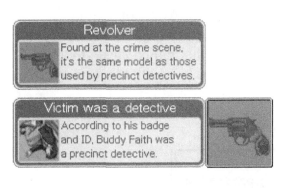

Now go into Logic mode and connect **Revolver** with **Victim was a detective**. Since the revolver is assigned to the detectives of the precinct and the victim is a detective, that means the gun was the victim's! Further examination of the body reveals an empty gun holster! The **Victim's Revolver** will be added to the Organizer. **Examine** the barrel of the gun to check the chamber. Looks like only one shot was fired from this gun.

Bad Ending 1: If your logic runs out here, Gumshoe thinks that you are too tired, so he takes over. As days go by, the case remains unresolved.

Suddenly, someone bursts into the room. He looks like the murderer! After wrongly accusing you and Gumshoe of killing "Jim" (which is what he calls his now-late partner Buddy Faith) he introduces himself as Jacques Portsman. After some more conversation, he will request that the officer dusting the framed jacket to take some pictures of him with his former friend.

Now you can **examine** the framed jacket that the officer was dusting. Immediately, you notice a contradiction!
The **Deduce** function is now introduced to you. **Highlight** the **bullet hole** on the frame and press ⊗ or the "Deduce" icon, then present the **Victim's Revolver**. Only one

bullet was fired from the gun, so how are there two bullet holes at the crime scene? There could only be **Another handgun**! You then remove the frame to reveal a **Secret Safe**! This is added to the Organizer. **Examine** the panel on the safe. Looks like someone used it and wiped the fingerprints clean! This gives you the **Wiped fingerprints** logic, and the **Secret Safe** will be updated in the Organizer.

Go into Logic mode and connect **The killer's goal** with **Wiped fingerprints**. Since the fingerprints on the safe were wiped off, the murderer might be trying to steal something! This gives you the **Motive: Theft (?)** logic. Now connect **Signs of a struggle** with **Motive: Theft (?)**. The mess of files might be the result of the killer searching the files, not a struggle between the killer and the victim! Gumshoe will rearrange the files with the help of Portsman.

Now **deduce** the **bullet hole** in the bottom right of the files and present the **Crime Scene Notes**. The victim was shot in the abdomen, and he was standing at the time based on the bloody handprints, so the bullet hole couldn't have been where the files are! When prompted, select **The order of the files**. The files must have been arranged incorrectly at the time of the crime. However, you say that the files are arranged as you left it, even though the name of the files are in the wrong order. So that means the files were arranged incorrectly by someone else at the time of the murder!

After rearranging the files, looks like your assumption was right! You will receive the **Files in disarray** logic. However, there will now be another thing that will catch your eye... **Examine** the **bloody files** at the bottom right previously concealed by the body, where you'll find the word "Gumshoe" written upside-down in blood! Or, at least, most of it; one of the files is stolen, too! The **Stolen File** will be added to the Organizer.

And with that, your investigation is complete!

Bad Ending 2: If you run out of logic here, Portsman claims he found the culprit and forces you to vacate the crime scene.

Confrontation

Now Portsman will once again accuse Gumshoe of killing Faith. You decide to cross-examine Portsman, as done in court. Gumshoe will ask how you do it. If you're an Ace Attorney veteran, you should know how to do this, so pick **Maybe some other time**. If this is your first time playing an Ace Attorney game, pick **Might as well**, and you will explain how it works to Gumshoe (scroll through statements with ⊕ or the arrow icons; present evidence on statements by pressing ⬚R⬚ or the "Present" icon, selecting evidence that contradicts the statement with ⊕ or ◼, then pressing Ⓧ or the "Present" icon again; press a statement for more info by pressing ⬚L⬚ or the "Press" icon).

Portsman's Argument: Mr. Portsman's Logic

1. Detective Gumshoe. You stole Jim's gun from him and shot him dead.

2. Furthermore, you messed up the files to make it look like you had committed theft instead.

3. That's when you moved Jim's body

7

that was sitting in front of the bookshelf!

4. But thanks to that, you didn't notice the bloody letters his body was hiding.

5. And it will be by his final words that you will be brought to justice.

Rebuttal: Mr. Portsman's Logic

Present the **Stolen File** on the **fourth statement**. If Gumshoe stole the file, he would've seen his name! The missing letters in Gumshoe's name also mean that the file was stolen after the murder!

Mr. Portsman is left speechless, but he still has something up his sleeve! He calls for a young lady of the building's security to be escorted here. Gumshoe starts to get mad at this. Looks like it's none other than Maggey Byrde, the security guard on shift that night. (Phoenix Wright fans should recognize her too!) She could have used the master key that opens all the building's doors to get in! It's time for another cross-examination.

Who's Maggie Byrde? Without spoiling anything, play Phoenix Wright: Ace Attorney - Justice For All and Trials and Tribulations to know the story behind her bad luck-stricken character.

Bad Ending 3: If you can't counter this argument, Portsman will arrest Gumshoe on the spot, leaving you in despair.

Portsman's Argument: Reason for Suspicion

1. It's pretty obvious that Ms. Byrde snuck into your room using the master key.

2. I mean, if Detective Gumshoe isn't the one who opened the door...

3. ...then that leaves only Ms. Byrde as our prime suspect.

4. On top of which, she knows our good detective, doesn't she?

5. Making it all the more probable that she was the one who faked the dying message.

After this, the **Master Key** will be added to the Organizer.

Rebuttal: Reason for Suspicion

Press the **first statement**. Maggey will say that she wasn't able to use the master key! Select **Ask for more details** when given the chance. She will say that the master key wasn't at the booth at 1 AM. Maggey will say that the key disappeared at 1 AM then magically reappeared after that! Portsman will add a statement into his testimony:

- Her intent? From the messed-up shelves to the wiped-down safe, I'd say thievery.

Present the **Secret Safe** at this statement. Only prosecutors know about the safe, so Maggey couldn't have been the thief! She couldn't have found it by accident either, as, going by the bookshelf and the safe, the thief knew exactly where to look. Looks like Portsman is cornered here. However, he suddenly claims that he told Faith about the safes, and comes up with a new theory:

Faith was the thief, and Maggey was just going to stop him, being a security guard. The victim stole the key, went into the office, got shot by Maggey in self-defense, and Maggey took the key back with her! Portsman will thus force you and Gumshoe out of the crime scene.

Bad Ending 4: Between this second argument and fourth argument on "Part 1-2 - End", Portsman arrests Byrde, claiming victory for Jim's soul. Before you can speak, Portsman says that no one would listen to you as the case is closed.

Part 1-2 - End

Investigation: Hallway

Begin by **examining** the **leftmost sofa**, and then **examine** the **object** under it. Looks like it's the stolen file! You explain to Gumshoe that it's a case from the previous prosecutor that used your office.
The **Stolen File** is updated to the **Stolen 0-Series File**. Now **talk** to Maggey:

- **The victim:** Seems like Faith played basketball with Portsman outside his office.
- **Maggey Byrde:** Maggey talks about her unlucky life. Nothing notable about this.

Now **present** the **Master Key** to Maggey. Nothing new, but Maggey's sure that the **Master key was stolen**. She also says that she recently used it! You have a new topic to talk about.

- **Used the master key?:** Maggey recalls that a prosecutor needed her help since he lost the key to his office. Then she remembers that it was Portsman! Talk about this new topic.
- **Forgetful Mr. Portsman:** Apparently, Portsman wanted her to open the door to his office for him, and he later called Maggey to close his office door as he returned at about 1:30 AM. But does that mean she really **Used the master key**?

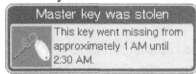
Master key was stolen
This key went missing from approximately 1 AM until 2:30 AM.

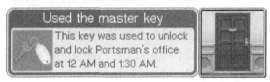
Used the master key
This key was used to unlock and lock Portsman's office at 12 AM and 1:30 AM.

Time for some logic! Connect **Master key was stolen** with **Used the master key**. You realize that she couldn't have used the master key at 1:30 AM because the master key was stolen! Maggey says that it was lost, but she didn't want to admit it, so she pretended to lock the door with her house key! That means Portsman's door must still be unlocked! **Mr. Portsman's Office** is added to your Organizer.

9

Now move to the right. Hey, there's Winston Payne from the previous games, offering us help! But that's not our concern here. **Examine** the **door** with the basketball hoop next to it; this must be Portsman's door. **Examine** the **doorknob**, and you note that it's locked. Wait, what? **Deduce** the **doorknob** and present **Mr. Portsman's Office**. Maggey didn't lock the door, so how is it locked tight? You say that to find out the reason, we must examine some fingerprints; select **Prints on the doorknob**. Looks like only Portsman and the victim's prints are on here, but there's one set of prints missing! Whose? **Present Maggey Byrde's profile**. If she unlocked this door, then shouldn't her prints be on this knob? **Mr. Portsman's Office** is updated in the Organizer. You then notice something and the view pans down.

Examine the **paper** sticking out from underneath the door. Looks like it's a note Faith left for Portsman; apparently, Faith brought some evidence Portsman had requested, but Portsman was out at the time.

The **Note Left by Victim** is added to the Organizer. Now **examine** the base of the **basketball hoop**. You notice that it's been moved. The **Basketball Hoop** is added to the Organizer. Now go and **examine** your **door**, then **examine** the **doorknob**. Looks like the door was unlocked with a key and the prints were wiped clean.

And with that, your investigation is complete!

Bad Ending 5: If you run out of logic here, Portsman steps out of your Office, announcing the investigation is over while also arresting Byrde and taking her away, leaving you speechless.

Second Confrontation

It's pretty obvious who's the criminal now. Prepare yourself, as you're going to confront the murderer, Jacques Portsman. Portsman isn't very keen on admitting his guilt, so you must force it out of him.

Portsman's Testimony: Mr. Portsman's Rebuttal

1. I have no idea what sort of hair-brained idea you have in mind, but...
2. ...there's a mountain of evidence that points away from me being the culprit.
3. Besides, how, may I ask, do you propose I unlocked your door and got in here?

4. Look, I feel bad doing this to you, but I've got work to do, so we're done here.

Rebuttal: Mr. Portsman's Rebuttal

Present the **Master Key** on the **third statement**. Portsman says that he never touched the key. However, he had another way of using it; **Present Maggey Byrde's profile**. You explain that the door Portsman asked Maggey to open was Edgeworth's, but Maggey herself says that she opened Portsman's. You rebut that Portsman could have easily exchanged the door plates, and he would have had another good way of tricking Maggey into thinking it was his office: **Present** the **Basketball Hoop**. Since it stands out so much in the hallway, it can leave a strong impression. Furthermore, there are marks at the base of the hoop that suggest it's been moved. However, Portsman claims it's all conjecture. Looks like its time for another cross-examination!

Portsman's Testimony: Conjecture's Rebuttal

1. Now you're just spouting nonsense.
2. I had the girl open my office door.
3. After that, I was in my room the entire time.
4. You don't have a single reason to suspect me!

Rebuttal: Conjecture's Rebuttal

Present the **Note Left by Victim** on the **third statement**. The note says that Portsman wasn't in his office when Faith arrived, meaning that Portsman was somewhere else during that time! However, Portsman asserts that Maggey opened the door to his office. **Present Mr. Portsman's Office**. Maggey's prints aren't on the doorknob, and your doorknob has been wiped clean! The victim must have heard noises from the opposite room upon coming in, went in, and saw Portsman, who shot him. By then, you came and were threatened by him! Portsman now says that your claim is too circumstantial and that he has a solid alibi. Let's hear what it is.

Bad Ending 6: If you run out of logic here, Portsman says that you are trying to pin the murder on yourself, believing it's a swing and a miss. Portsman also says that unless there's evidence to disprove his alibi, he'll take Maggey into custody.

Portsman's Testimony: Portsman's Alibi

1. If memory serves, you came back to this office at around 2 AM, correct?
2. And it was then that you had that unfortunate confrontation at gunpoint with the culprit.
3. But at exactly that time, I was down in Criminal Affairs!
4. Ask around. I'm sure the other detectives will corroborate my story. It's the perfect alibi!

Rebuttal: Portsman's Alibi

Perfect alibi, indeed. Unfortunately, there aren't any contradictions here, so **press** everything for now. You have nothing to work with, but you do receive the **Mr. Portsman's alibi** logic.

You will automatically enter Logic mode. Connect **Mr. Portsman's alibi** with **Another handgun**. There were two bullets shot that night, but only one shot from the murder weapon. The killer had to use the victim's gun, so he couldn't have prepared another gun. That means there must've been **Another visitor**! Connect this with **Files in disarray**. The files could have been rearranged by these two different people, one before the murder and one after. You explain the whole sequence of the murder, but Portsman cries "*Objection!*", now saying that the second person should be the prime suspect.

Portsman's Testimony: Portsman's Alibi, Pt. 2

1. That thief you ran into should be your real suspect, wouldn't you say?
2. We should be out there looking for that thief right now. They might still be nearby.
3. I hate to repeat myself, but as I've already said, I was training in my room.
4. And when Jim came to deliver some evidence to me, I was down at Criminal Affairs.
5. So I can't be expected to know what happened around here after I left.

Rebuttal: Portsman's Alibi, Pt. 2

Press the **fourth statement**. Faith brought two things from a previous case, a gun and a pendant. Portsman will add this statement to his testimony:

- He brought me two items, a gun and a pendant, that are related to yesterday's case.

Present the **Note Left by Victim** at this new statement. Portsman claims he only brought two pieces of evidence, but the note says three! Portsman hid a piece of evidence! You order Gumshoe to search him. And he finds... a **Video Tape**. However, something is interesting on this tape. **Examine** the **bloodstain** at the back of the tape. The blood is still fresh, so it could be the victim's! Portsman chews on his medal, breaks down, and faints.

What really happened

Jacques Portsman wanted to steal something from Miles Edgeworth's office. He knew Edgeworth was out, but he didn't have the key to the door. Thus, he hatched a plan: he moved his basketball hoop outside Edgeworth's office and swapped the room plates, then requested for Maggey Byrde, the security guard on shift at the time, to open the door for him. Maggey, not knowing that it was Edgeworth's door, opened it with the master key. Portsman entered and started his search, looking through the files, which he rearranged wrongly afterwards, and the secret safe.

At this time, Portsman's partner, Buddy Faith, arrived at the hallway, bringing with him three pieces of evidence that Portsman had requested: a gun, a pendant, and a tape. Finding that Portsman wasn't in his office, he left a note for him under the door. However, he suddenly heard noises coming from Edgeworth's office next door... the office whose occupant was out at the time. Suspecting a thief, he grabbed the master key from the guard booth and entered the office, only to catch his partner red-handed within. After a brief conversation, Portsman snatched Faith's gun from him and shot him, silencing the sole witness to his crime. However, Faith's blood splattered onto the tape that Faith was holding. Thinking quickly, Portsman wrote Gumshoe's name with Faith's blood to pin the crime on him. Exiting the room and taking the master key and the bloodstained tape from Faith with him, he requested that Maggey close the door for him. Maggey, who couldn't find the master key, pretended to lock Edgeworth's door with her house key. Once Maggey left, Portsman wiped the doorknob clean to conceal his presence there, and returned the master key to the guard booth, before going down to Criminal Affairs to establish an alibi.

Sometime later, another thief came to steal something from Edgeworth's office and found that the door was unlocked, and helped themselves in. Though they found Faith's body, they ignored it, and stole the 0-series file they were looking for, rearranging the files correctly in the process. This is when Edgeworth returned to his office. Hearing Edgeworth coming, the thief hid. Entering his office, Edgeworth was greeted by the smell of blood, and quickly discovered Faith's body, but was suddenly held at gunpoint by the thief. Assuming this person was the murderer, Edgeworth vowed that no one would get away with murder in his office. In response, the thief turned and fired a round, almost hitting Edgeworth's jacket but knocking its frame down. The thief then escaped, taking some pages from the file and leaving it under a sofa in the hallway. Edgeworth then called the authorities to report the murder.

Epilogue

Maggey thanks you for proving her innocence. Gumshoe notes that there were rumors that Portsman was corrupt, doing things like forging evidence and not taking cases for vague reasons. Gumshoe also mentions rumors that a huge organization is behind this. This will become important in the future. You say that one piece of evidence didn't have any significance; present the **Stolen 0-Series File**. It is not known what the thief was up to and why they only stole some pages of the file. Just then, an officer will give Edgeworth something he found in his office: a card with a raven mark on it. You and Gumshoe both recognize it; it's the calling card of the Yataragatsu - a famously methodical thief that steals evidence from corruption from major companies and presents it to the press. You then mention how this relates to a case from two days ago…

TURNABOUT AIRLINES

Part 2-1 - Beginning

You get up from the floor of the first-floor lounge of a fancy aeroplane, dazed. Checking your watch, you realize you have been unconscious for ten minutes due to recent turbulence. The pilot then announces that the plane will hit more turbulence soon. As you head towards the elevator to return to your first-class seat, something falls out of your pocket. It's a travel wallet dripping with grape juice, but it's not yours. Now you face two of your worst fears: earthquake-like turbulence and an elevator. Those who played Phoenix Wright: Ace Attorney might remember the story behind this. As you open the door, you see... a body?! Suddenly, a flight attendant approaches and accuses you of murder! The plane then hits more turbulence and you faint again.

Sometime later, on the second floor of the plane, the flight attendant introduces herself as Rhoda Teneiro. Looks like the passengers know what happened, and yet she tied you up! Teneiro says that you're

under suspicion of the murder and that she has incriminating evidence. Looks like we're starting to have a confrontation session with Ms. Teneiro right off the bat. Time to prove your innocence right away!

Teneiro's Testimony: What Ms. Teneiro Saw

1. I swear to tell the whole truth as a professional flight attendant.
2. Unfortunately for you, Mr. Edgeworth, I am certain you are the killer.
3. The scene I saw in front of the elevator...
4. ...it was you, standing there, with fresh blood dripping off of the murder weapon.
5. So, if you would please cooperate, we'll turn you over just as soon as we land.

Rebuttal: What Ms. Teneiro Saw

Present the **Travel Wallet** at the **fourth statement**. The "murder weapon" that she saw was the travel wallet you found! The "blood" that was dripping from it is actually grape juice! Teneiro is still persistent that you killed the victim and she asks to examine the wallet. **Examine** the **gold button** to open the wallet. There's only a passport inside! But the owner of that passport is the victim, Akbey Hicks! The **Travel Wallet** is updated to **Mr. Hicks's Travel Wallet**.

With this new information, Teneiro accuses you of theft now.

Teneiro's Argument: Ms. Teneiro's Logic

1. As you claimed, the murder weapon is not the travel wallet...
2. ...however, it IS something you stole from Mr. Hicks after you were done with the vile deed.
3. I find it hard to believe myself, but your motive was very simple...
4. You were out to steal Mr. Hicks' money, weren't you?

Rebuttal: Ms. Teneiro's Logic

This murder wasn't because of money. Present the **Crime Scene Notes** at **statement 4** (alternatively, you may present the **Travel Wallet** then the **Crime Scene Notes** and bypass the next line, but it is not necessary). To prove why she's wrong, present the **bills on the floor.** The floor is scattered with money, but the killer didn't take them! Convinced that you have pleaded a strong case for your innocence, Teneiro releases you.

Suddenly, a man speaking an unknown language walks up. Looks like he's Borginian (we've seen people from this country before in Apollo Justice: Ace Attorney), but he can speak English as well. He wants you under arrest until the plane touches down. After whining about wasting his precious time, he introduces himself as Zinc Lablanc II, and he is an art dealer. He says he saw the victim go down to the lounge at about 6 o'clock! Teneiro discovered the body at 6:15, so that means the victim would have been killed within this 15-minute timespan. And the only person at the lounge was you! Lablanc says that he saw the man the whole time operating his cell phone.

You request an investigation of the crime scene, and we have the captain's approval! All right, begin investigation!

Bad Ending One: If you fail your logic before the investigation, Teneiro accuses you of ruining the passengers' fun, and refuses to let you plead your case any further. You get arrested upon landing.

Investigation: Lounge

Move left and you will be in the **First Floor - Lounge**. You thank Teneiro for permitting you to access the crime scene. As she reminds you, however, you're not off the hook yet; since you were the only one in the lounge, you are the prime suspect. You automatically move to Hicks' body.

You know you aren't the killer, so that means the killer must be somewhere else here... so **Where was the killer?**

Examine the **Elevator**. It seems that the only accessible floors are the first and second, but Teneiro explains that you can also go to the cargo area with a keycard.

Examine the **brown thing** at the bottom right-hand corner of the elevator. It seems to be a piggy bank modeled after the airline's bear mascot, but there is blood on it. You receive the **Murder weapon: Mr. Ifly?** logic.

Examine the **body**. It looks Hicks was hit by the back of the head; in other words, **Blunt force trauma**. He also has **Broken glasses**, for some reason.

Examine the **paper** in Hicks' pocket. It's actually a picture of him in some building, in front of a statue in Borginia. The **Photo of Mr. Hicks** is added to the Organizer. Now **Deduce** the lanyard and **Present** the **Photo of Mr. Hicks**; his

cell phone on his lanyard seems to be missing. The **Missing Cell Phone** is added to the Organizer.

Now **examine** the **Spilled grape juice** near the statue. When prompted to choose what's strange here, select the **footprints** of grape juice just near the spill.

Time for some logic. Go into Logic mode and combine **Where was the killer?** and **Elevator**. It seems the killer could only be in the elevator with Hicks.

You get the **In the elevator with Hicks?** Logic.

Next, combine **Blunt force trauma** and **Murder weapon: Mr. Ifly?** Logically, there can only be one connection between the two: Mr. Ifly is the murder weapon. The **Mr. Ifly Piggy Bank** is added to the Organizer.

Now combine **In the elevator with Hicks?** and **Spilled grape juice**. It seems that the only reason there are footprints is that there was someone with Hicks in the elevator! **Grape Juice Footprints** are added to the Organizer. With that, your investigation is complete!

Bad Ending Two: If you run out of logic here, you beg Lablanc for more time, but Lablanc refuses. Teneiro reports to the captain about your lack of progress and you are arrested upon landing.

Lablanc's Testimony: What I Saw

1. I am certain I saw Mr. Hicks in the elevator!
2. It was when my needles on my pocket watch pointed to the 6 and to the 12!
3. The body was discovered 15 minutes after that in the lounge, yes?
4. Then you, the only person in the lounge at that time, must be the criminal!

Rebuttal: What I Saw

Press the **first statement**. A new statement is added:

- The only person inside was that Mr. Hicks man!

Present the **Grape Juice Footprints** on that **statement**. You've already inferred that there was another person in the elevator. However, Lablanc insists there were no other people in the elevator. He doesn't seem to be lying, so what does it mean?

Lablanc's Testimony: What I Saw, Pt.2

1. I was very upset when Mr. Hicks passed by my seat.
2. I was checking the time, over and over again.
3. I happened to follow that man with my eyes when he passed me.
4. And I saw clearly into the elevator he was entering.
5. But, I swear there was no one else inside! No one!

Rebuttal: What I Saw Pt.2

Press the **second statement**. Lablanc wanted to watch a movie not available in his country, but according to him, it never showed. He adds two statements:

- The movie I wanted to see would

not start, so I checked my pocket watch many times.

- My watch is set to my destination's time. I always set it when I board the plane.

Present the **Sky Magazine** on the second of the new statements. It seems that the plane has not changed the time to their destination's timezone. So that means the difference between the time zone of Borginia and our country is 9 hours - therefore, Lablanc saw Hicks at around 3 AM! So Hicks could have been killed at any time between 3 AM and 6:15 AM.

Now the other attendant speaks up. She introduces herself as Cammy Meele and states she noted that the victim was in his seat at 5 AM when the plane stopped to refuel in a country called the Republic of Zheng Fa. No-one got on board or left the plane during the refueling. Information regarding the **Refueling in Zheng Fa** is added to the Organizer. Cammy also claims that Hicks was in his seat when the plane took off again at 5 AM. **Ms. Meele's Testimony** is added to the Organizer. Now the timeframe of the murder can be narrowed down to sometime between 5 AM and 6:15 AM. But you were in the lounge during this time period!

The only way to prove your innocence is to prove that the crime happened in another location. **Present** the **Grape Juice**

Footprints. The footprints lead to the in-flight shop, but they are disconnected. However, there is another piece of evidence that can connect the shop to the crime scene. **Present** the **Mr. Ifly Piggy Bank**. The murder weapon is a piece of merchandise sold at the in-flight shop, so the criminal must have obtained it there. Teneiro will confirm it was in the shop at 5:40 AM. But that's just before the patch of turbulence!

She also reveals that when you found the body, she had just exited the flight attendant's room. This means she was also on the first floor around the time of the murder! Teneiro claims that she had to go to the in-flight shop before going to the flight attendant's room, passing by you as you were reading the airline magazine. As the murder weapon is confirmed to be at the shop around the time of the murder, that means we must investigate it. However, Cammy reminds us that we don't have the captain's permission to enter the in-flight shop yet. While Teneiro claims that she asked for the captain's permission to investigate the whole plane, Cammy says that the captain didn't grant any permission at all.

It's obvious now that Teneiro was lying and she's called to the cockpit. However, Cammy already got permission from the captain to search the shop. Walk right into the shop. The shop's a big mess. Since the murder weapon came from here, that means the killer must have visited this place. You receive the **Murder weapon: Mr. Ifly** logic.

Investigation: In-Flight Shop

First, **examine** the **cupboard** with the shattered glass door. There is nothing on display except for a **Tiny captain's hat**. You feel like you've seen it somewhere before...

Now, **examine** the bright yellow **suitcases**. Seems like they are designed by Teneiro, but not one **Suitcase** has ever been sold. Suddenly, a patch of turbulence causes the suitcase to roll to the other side of the room. That is very dangerous, and something worth noting too.

Now enter Logic mode and connect **Murder weapon: Mr. Ifly** with **Tiny captain's hat**. Seems like the hat probably belongs on the piggy bank's head. It's possible that this piggy bank was forcibly removed from its case, dropping its hat. The **Mr. Ifly Piggy Bank** is updated in your organizer.

Since we now know that the killer could have broken the glass case to get the murder weapon, we can now take a closer look at the shattered glass case. **Deduce** the **empty shelf** and present the **Mr. Ifly Piggy Bank**. If the killer broke the glass to get the piggy bank, then why is there no glass at all in the shelf where it was displayed? That means that the display case was broken from the inside out, meaning the piggy bank must've fallen out of the case during a patch of turbulence! The hat could've also been knocked off its head. This means the killer took the murder weapon after the patch of **Turbulence** that caused it to fall out of the case. The **Mr.**

Ifly Piggy Bank is updated in your Organizer. Since the murder happened before the turbulence, this means that the piggy bank was picked up after the murder. The piggy bank isn't the murder weapon!

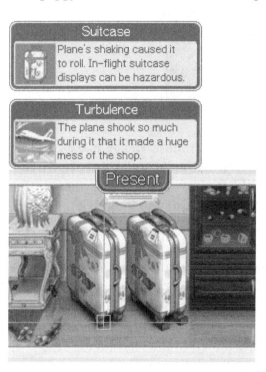

Cammy presents another possibility: the killer could have broken the glass case to get the murder weapon and do it from inside out even if the case is locked. The only person that could have done that is Teneiro. Since she is responsible for the shop's upkeep, she has the keys to the case.

Now go into Logic mode and connect **Suitcase** with **Turbulence**. If these suitcases were so prone to moving when the plane shakes, why is it the only thing undisturbed in this shop? You now enter a close-up shot of the suitcases.

There's something wrong with these suitcases. **Present** the **front wheels of the**

left suitcase. The right suitcase has stoppers to prevent it from moving, but the left suitcase has none. Without it, the suitcase couldn't have stayed in the same spot. So, it must have been placed here after the patch of turbulence!

You will now examine the suitcase itself. **Examine** the peculiar **purple wheel**. Looks like it's covered in grape juice, but why? Now **examine** the **lock**. It's unlocked, so you can open it up. What's inside is a blood-stained cloth. The suitcase could have been used by the murderer to move something... such as the victim's body. To confirm this, **present** the **Crime Scene Notes**. The **Ifly Suitcase** and **Bloody Cloth** are added to the Organizer. This could mean that the murder happened somewhere else and the body was moved into the elevator by the killer. Teneiro said she was here for "work-related matters". Could she have been behind this...?

Teneiro then returns and says that you have no more time to investigate. You can still watch over the preservation of the site until the plane touches down, however. While you may have proven your innocence, the mystery isn't solved!

Bad Ending Three: If you run out of logic here, Cammy will ask the captain to halt the investigation and forces you back to your seat.

Part 2-2 - Middle

Now that the plane's back on the ground, local police will take over the investigation. A familiar face then approaches: it's Franziska von Karma, the daughter of your mentor, Manfred von Karma. But it seems she thinks that you are the killer! She won't let you investigate the crime for now, and Detective Gumshoe's called over to watch over you. **Talk** to him:

- **Initial Investigation:** Looks like the investigation was already underway as soon as the plane arrived. Curiously, Franziska was already here before Gumshoe even got there. And she was supposed to be in Germany, so what brought her here?
- **Franziska von Karma:** Franziska already arrived in America to investigate a certain "top-secret" incident.

A hidden Easter egg: If you check with one of the people sitting on the right, you'll notice Sal Manella as one of the people. You'll remember him from Turnabout Samurai in the first game, as he's the director of the "Steel Samurai".

Now that you know why Franziska is here, you should resume your investigation. Walk left back into the plane. Seems like Franziska is questioning the captain; better not interrupt her. You will go down to the first-floor lounge.

Bad Ending Four: If your logic ends here, Franziska stops the investigation.

Despite Gumshoe's protests, you get arrested on the spot.

Seems like Lablanc is causing a commotion. If you talk to the officer, he tells you that you can't enter the flight attendant's room. **Talk** to Lablanc. Apparently, he needs to retrieve his cargo, but since the police aren't done investigating, he can't do that.

- **Lablanc's cargo:** Lablanc has a collection of different art pieces in the cargo hold.

Present the **Bloody Cloth**. It has the same pattern as Lablanc's hat. Turns out it is made with Borginian cloth and is one of Borginia's world-famous exports. The **Bloody Cloth** is updated in the Organizer to the **Borginian Cloth**. Lablanc also mentions that the flight attendant hasn't come out of the flight attendant's room for a while. That could only mean that Teneiro is in there.

- **Rhoda Teneiro:** Apparently, Teneiro is still being questioned in the flight attendant's room.

Franziska then appears and requests that you prove your innocence. If you succeed, she will let you enter the flight attendant's room. Looks like it's time for a confrontation!

Franziska's Argument: Franziska's Logic

1. Let's not complicate things and go with the most obvious conclusion.

21

2. The scene of the crime was here, in the very lounge the body was discovered.
3. From the time the victim was seen calling for an attendant until his body as found...
4. ...the only person in this lounge the entire time was you, Miles Edgeworth!
5. This, unmistakably, makes you the likeliest suspect.

Rebuttal: Franziska's Logic

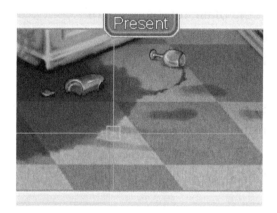

Present the **Ifly Suitcase** on the **second statement**. The suitcase was used to move the body to the elevator, meaning the crime scene wasn't in the lounge! Franziska claims that the suitcase could've simply been used to hide the cloth, not move the body. That is possible, but the suitcase was definitely moved. **Present** the **Grape Juice Footprints** and then **present** the **two lines leading away from the grape juice**. Grape juice was also found on the wheels of the suitcase, so the suitcase was used to move the body! But Franziska insists you still haven't proven your innocence just yet.

Franziska's Argument: Franziska's Logic, Pt. 2

1. You prepared yourself and acquired the piggy bank before the plane hit that turbulence.
2. And then, you waited for the victim in the lounge, where you beat him to death.
3. Then, while you were in the elevator with the victim's body stuck in the suitcase...
4. ...the plane hit the patch of turbulence, and out flew the body from within the suitcase!
5. With no way out, you hastily put the suitcase back where you had taken it from...
6. ...and pretended to be the "discoverer" of the body.

Rebuttal: Franziska's Logic, Pt. 2

This is way too easy. **Present** the **Mr. Ifly Piggy Bank** on the **first statement**. We know that the piggy bank could only be taken from the shop *after* the turbulence, and the blood could be added after the murder. The killer probably picked the bank up after returning the suitcase to its original location once the murder was committed, to fabricate the murder weapon, before planting the victim's travel wallet in your pocket to pin the crime on you.

There aren't any other objects resembling a murder weapon found on the plane and the best place to hide a murder weapon will logically be in the suitcase with the cloth. That means either the murder weapon is still being carried by the murderer or it's still on this very plane. Franziska presents a third possibility: the murder weapon *was* the piggy bank, and was obtained by someone unlocking the display case and taking it, breaking the glass case at the same time. That means the killer must have had the key to the display case, which could mean Teneiro did it! That's not all, as she pretended to have been permitted to help you investigate the plane. Franziska allows you into the flight attendant's room. Looks like we can move forward with our investigation.

Attendant's Room

Teneiro is still here. **Talk** to her:

- **Captain's permission:** Teneiro only lied about getting permission because she knew the captain will only listen to Cammy.
- **In-flight shop:** Teneiro only went to the shop to check the stock and went to the flight attendant's room after that.

Present the **Ifly Suitcase**. Teneiro designed the suitcase and was also the reason she went to the in-flight shop. She only went there to see how her suitcases were selling and was glad to see there was one last suitcase remaining... wait, what? There's no way that can be right!

- **The last suitcase:** Teneiro clearly remembers that only one suitcase was in the shop when she checked it, but there was two while you were investigating!

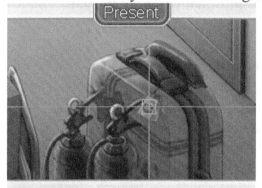

You notice another suitcase in the room. Teneiro clarifies it's hers and she had been using it for a long time. But that can't be right. **Present** the **price tag** on the suitcase. Why is it still there if Teneiro had been using it for a long time? The suitcase could only have been taken from the **in-flight shop** and the person who took it was **Rhoda Teneiro**. Teneiro took the suitcase to this room simply to make it look like it was selling well, when in reality it isn't, so she buys one for every flight she works. She presents the **Suitcase Receipt** with a timestamp of 5:40 AM, which is added to the Organizer. All of these suitcases are going to be scrapped at the end of this flight and they are all in the cargo hold, so the killer could have used one of the suitcases there.

Other than the elevator, the cargo hold can be accessed from a door in the flight attendant's room. There is no special lock

because only personnel holding a certain keycard can actually enter the flight attendant's room. That leaves out all the passengers and narrows down the suspects to all the crew members. Franziska notes that since the killer used the elevator when moving the body, they must have a different keycard to use the elevator. One that only Teneiro has! She claims it's missing but she could simply be hiding it. Teneiro is arrested and the chapter will end.

Bad Ending Five: If you run out of logic here, Franziska arrests Teneiro as a valuable witness.

Part 2-3 - End 1

Investigation: Cargo Hold

Examine the yellow **suitcases**. There is clearly one missing, as well as some **Glass shards** near them.

Next, **examine** the **black suitcase**. Looks like this is Hicks', and he has... a **Profile on Franziska**? Strange... did Hicks know her?

Talk to Franziska. She was already at the airport when the airplane landed, giving out orders. But why?

- **Why at the airport?:** Franziska was investigating a large multi-national crime, and has collaborated with **Interpol**.

Now we can start connecting some logic pieces! First, connect the **Glass shards** with the **Broken glasses**. The glass shards are the broken lens of

Hicks' glasses, meaning he was here. Now connect the **Profile on Franziska** with **Interpol**. Hicks could've been an agent of Interpol who was supposed to meet up with Franziska at the airport. Looks like we have some questions for Franziska. **Talk** to her again:

- **Truth about Hicks:** She confirms that Hicks was an Interpol agent investigating an international **Smuggling** ring. He was supposed to call Franziska when he landed.

Agent Hicks must have come down to the cargo hold as part of his investigation, but since he couldn't have had the keycard, he could have been accompanied by a crew member. Once he was there, the killer killed him and moved his body into the elevator. As the plane hit the patch of turbulence, the victim's body flew out of the suitcase along with his belongings. And with that, our investigation is complete!

All this evidence seems to point to Teneiro... or does it? Franziska seems to think so, and she presents her argument.

Franziska's Argument: Definitive Evidence

1. If it was a crew member, any one of them could've shown Agent Hicks to the cargo hold.
2. But the point to keep in mind is the keycard that allows the elevator to come down here.

3. The only person with such high-level access is Ms. Rhoda Teneiro!
4. I'd say that's a pretty decisive piece of information, wouldn't you?

Rebuttal: Definitive Evidence

Press the **second statement**. Teneiro claimed her keycard was stolen, so it is possible someone else did it. Franziska rebuts that she's the only person who can get the murder weapon from the locked display. You get a new statement.

- Further, there is the matter of the key to the display case that held the murderous bank.

Press this new **statement**. It might not be the murder weapon, but Franziska doesn't accept that. There is no other possible murder weapon. We must find a way to rule the piggy bank out and we can do that by further examining **the body**. We don't even know the victim's autopsy reports, so how can we be sure that his death was caused by the piggy bank?

Cause of death
Extensive bruising from back of head down to mid-back, as if severely beaten.

Mr. Ifly piggy bank
Is there some way for me to prove that this isn't the real murder weapon?

Weapon couldn't be found
Nobody could find anything that could be considered the real weapon in the hold.

A sizable weapon
The unusually large area of bruising suggests that a very large weapon was used!

Franziska orders Gumshoe to get the autopsy report. He returns, but with some bad news. The victim died by a blow to his head but was bruised from his shoulder to his mid-back. The **Autopsy Report** is added to the Organizer. But this doesn't answer how Agent Hicks died...

At that moment, Lablanc barges into the cargo hold trying to check on his luggage. And he's willing to do that by force! Running straight at the officer, he bounces off... and stumbles over the railing! This causes you to have a revelation as he falls, and you recall the facts: you need to prove that the **Mr. Ifly piggy bank** isn't the real murder weapon, the real murder **Weapon couldn't be found** and the **Cause of death** was from extensive bruising from the victim's head to his mid-back.

You automatically enter Logic mode. Connect **Cause of death** with **Mr. Ifly piggy bank**. It's only one bruise down the victim's back; since the piggy bank is too

25

small for that, **A sizeable weapon** would be needed instead. Now connect **Weapon couldn't be found** with **A sizeable weapon**. A large weapon would have been discovered ages ago, so why haven't we found anything like it? Unless it's something so big we completely missed it. However, we **don't have evidence to show** it. The cause of death was not caused by a beating, it was caused by a **free fall**! Hicks fell to his death! That explains the size of his injuries. The victim fell from the top of the stairs down to the floor of the cargo hold.

That means... oh no, Lablanc may also be dead! Fortunately not, as he's alive and still conscious. If that large piece of cargo hadn't been there to break his fall, he would've died... This proves that Agent Hicks could have been killed when the cargo box wasn't there. **Present Refueling in Zheng Fa**. The plane made a refueling in Zheng Fa, during which cargo was also transferred. The box next to it is labeled the Zheng Fa Express, so it was loaded after the refueling. The **Cargo from Zheng Fa** is added to the Organizer. Looks like it's time for another investigation.

Second Investigation: Cargo Hold

Examine the **large piece of cargo** that broke Lablanc's fall. It turns out this is part of Lablanc's cargo. We could get more information about it from him. **Talk** to Lablanc:

- **Lablanc's Cargo:** The cargo contains the "Alif Red Statue" from Europe, and it's a quite **Valuable piece of art**. In fact, it's too valuable for us to investigate.

Now go into Logic mode and connect **Smuggling** with the **Valuable piece of art**. This statue could be a fake, transferred onto the ship during the refueling at Zheng Fa. **Talk** to Lablanc again:

- **Fake Statue:** Lablanc insists that his statue isn't a fake, presenting a Cargo Certification document to prove it. It was loaded on the plane back on Europe. This doesn't look good for our case... The **Alif Red Certificate** is added to the Organizer.

Lablanc finally reveals the statue. It seems pretty familiar, doesn't it? The **Alif Red Statue** is added to the Organizer.
Now **examine** the **statue**. Something in here contradicts something we already have. **Deduce** the **statue's eyes** and **present** the **Photo of Mr. Hicks**. The statue in the photo clearly has *red* eyes, but this statue has *orange* eyes... this statue is a fake! Now, move to the lower half of the statue. **Deduce** the **cloth stuck underneath the statue** and **present** the **Cargo from Zheng Fa**. If the neighboring piece of cargo was brought onto the plane at Zheng Fa, it couldn't have got its cloth stuck under the

statue if it was loaded in Europe! It was smuggled on in Zheng Fa.

Agent Hicks could've been investigating this statue. Even if he could've done that after the plane had landed, the cargo would have been swapped, implicating that the owner himself swapped it. That means someone was involved with forging the cargo certificates... The **Alif Red Certificate** is updated in the Organizer.

And with that, our investigation is complete. Agent Hicks likely knew that the Alif Red Statue was going to be smuggled, so he took the photo for future reference. Then, trying to find proof that the cargo was indeed smuggled, he came down to take a photo of the cargo hold. There wasn't any statue on the plane during this time, which alone could be good enough proof. He could then have had the cargo crew arrested for smuggling the statue.

After moving the statue, it's discovered that there is, in fact, blood under it. The killer did a good job cleaning it up, and they did it with a **Borginian Cloth** - otherwise, the cargo crew at Zheng Fa would discover the blood traces. Which means the murder could have happened before the plane landed to refuel. This means a certain person isn't telling the truth... **Ms. Meele's testimony** is contradictory. She claimed that the victim was still alive when the plane finished refueling, which means she must be lying. And we need to get the truth out of her.

Bad Ending Six: If your logic runs out here before Hick's cell phone is found,

26

Franziska ends the investigation prematurely, stating Teneiro's guilt to be obvious and that she'll be tried as a valuable witness.

Part 2-4 - End 2

Meele's Testimony: Ms. Meele's Alibi

1. ....Mnngh. Oh, um... yeah...
2. From 3 to 4, I was, um... in the flight attendant's room all by my lonesome self.
3. ....Mnngh. Oh, um... yeah...
4. And from 5 to 6, I was, um... in the flight attendant's room all by my lonesome self.

Well, ain't that helpful? Looks like you'll have to press her as she sleeps through her testimony! Someone has to wake her up so she can answer to the investigation…

Rebuttal: Ms. Meele's Alibi

Present the **Suitcase Receipt** on the **4th statement**. Alternatively, **Press** the **4th statement**. Cammy insists she was the only one in the flight attendant's room. **Raise an objection** and present the **Suitcase Receipt**. She couldn't have been the only one in the room, as Teneiro bought a suitcase and brought it to the room at around 5:40! Teneiro herself confirms that Cammy wasn't in the room. Her excuse? She went to the bathroom. Unfortunately, as unlikely

as that sounds, you can't prove she didn't! Cammy gives another testimony.

Meele's Testimony: Reason for Suspicion

1. Look, I know you're suspecting me 'cause I'm one of the crew.
2. But you'd think then maybe you should suspect Ms. Rhoda, too.
3. She's the one in charge of the elevator keycard and the shop, you know.
4. If you ask me, that makes her super-suspicious.

Rebuttal: Reason for Suspicion

Press the **3rd statement**. Cammy knows several languages to help passengers who can't speak English, and one of these languages happen to be Borginian. You get a new statement.

- All I'm in charge of are the attendants' room and some Borginian stuff.

Present the **Alif Red Certificate** at this **statement**. The document is falsified, and if she is the only person who speaks Borginian, it could've been done by none other than Cammy! She must have played a part in the smuggling of the statue! Cammy finally wakes up and reveals her true self but still denies participating in the smuggling. She then notes that Teneiro is much more likely to be a smuggling ring member, having access to a lot of the plane. You rebut that this is simply the killer trying to pin the murder on her and that they have been trying to do that from the beginning. When asked to prove how, **Present** the **Ifly Suitcase**. Out of all the places to hide a body, the killer chose to hide it in a suitcase. The killer didn't need to move the body to the first floor unless they were pinning the murder on Teneiro. Since she buys a suitcase on every flight, if the suitcase was swapped with the one with the body, it would implicate Teneiro as the killer. The sudden patch of turbulence ruined the plan and the killer tried to pin it on you. The killer then moved the suitcase to the in-flight shop and took the piggy bank to make a false murder weapon.

There is a special circumstance that required the killer to frame it on someone else, though, and that is **Where the murder took place**. Specifically, it took place in a plane in the air. The body wouldn't take long to be discovered, so the killer had to frame it on someone else. And that means only Cammy could've done it! Cammy states that all of this is just circumstantial evidence. She's right, but there's still one piece of evidence that never seemed to fit in the theory... **Present** the **Missing Cell Phone**. The killer must have taken the phone, so whoever has it must be the murderer. Cammy claims that the phone will have broken from the fall, so you ask Franziska to call the victim's phone number. The constant beeping of the phone can be heard, but where is it coming from?

Walk upstairs to enter the Flight Attendant's Room. The sound is much louder, so it must be here. **Examine** the **opened locker**. Looks like it's in Teneiro's locker. This is looking bad for Teneiro... very, very bad. Better do something fast before she gets arrested! The killer must've hidden the phone because it contained incriminating evidence. You automatically examine the phone. **Examine** the **camera lens**. The phone should be able to take pictures related to the smuggling case! The screens are broken, but even though we can't check the data, this means the killer couldn't have erased anything important. A quick data transfer to Franziska's phone reveals a photo of the Cargo Hold... without the statue! That's still not enough to convict Cammy, so we must do one last examination.

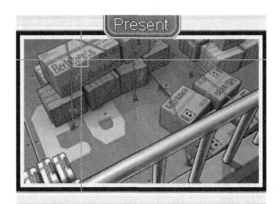

Bad Ending Seven: If your logic fails here, Cammy leaves under the pretense of working under another flight, and is never seen or heard of again.

Examine the **pile of boxes** where the Zheng Fa cargo and/or statue should be. They were shipped from Borginia to Zheng Fa, meaning the photo was taken before the refueling. Lablanc reveals that the boxes contain cloth. There's one piece of evidence we can tie to the killer, and that is the **Borginian Cloth**! The cloth was used to wipe up the blood, but it could only be obtained before the refueling. The labels are written in Borginian, so only a person fluent in Borginian could have opened one and used its contents, and the only crew member that knows Borginian is Cammy! While she states that the killer could have chanced upon the cloth after frantically searching the boxes, that is not possible. **Present** the **box labeled Bedsheets**. If the killer didn't know Borginian, they would have opened the box labeled "Bedsheets" right away, as bedsheets would have been perfect for cleaning up blood. The killer didn't want anyone to realize the crime scene was in the cargo hold, so they used the Borginian cloth to clean up the blood because it was to be unloaded in Zheng Fa.

With no way out, Cammy breaks down and confess to the crime.

What really happened

An international smuggling ring had set its sights on the Alif Red Statue. They had one of their members, Cammy Meele, help fake a document stating that the statue had been loaded on to the flight at Borginia. In reality, the statue was already smuggled off. Interpol suspected something was going on and sent one of their agents, Akbey Hicks, to investigate. Agent Hicks went to an exhibition of the statue and took a picture of it as a reference. He also booked the flight on which the businessman who owns

the statue, Zinc Lablanc, was on. Franziska von Karma was also notified to travel back to America to meet up with Hicks when he arrived.

A while after the plane took off and started cruising, Hicks decided to check out the cargo hold. He went down to the first floor using the elevator, passing by an annoyed Lablanc waiting for his in-flight movie at the wrong time. Meeting Cammy, he asked her to take him to the cargo hold. Using the entrance from the flight attendant's room, they entered the cargo hold atop the stairs. There, Hicks got a clear view of the cargo hold, finding that the Alif Red Statue was nowhere to be seen, and started taking pictures with his phone camera.

Being a member of the smuggling ring and panicking over the realization that she could be arrested once Interpol started investigating the missing statue, Cammy pushed Hicks over the railing and to the ground several feet below, killing him instantly and shattering his glasses, as well as his phone's LCD screens. Realizing what she had done, Cammy knew that she had to pin the crime on someone else. First, she cleaned the blood from the fall using the Borginian cloth, knowing that it would be unloaded during the Zheng Fa refueling. Then she took the victim's phone, knowing that it contained incriminating evidence about the smuggling, but couldn't erase it due to the broken screens.

Remembering that her colleague Rhoda Teneiro buys a suitcase from the shop on every flight, she used one of the suitcases in the cargo hold to move the body. She planned to exchange it with the suitcase Rhoda bought to divert suspicion onto her, but the body was too heavy to be carried up the staircase. Thus, she went back to the flight attendant's room, stole Teneiro's elevator keycard, and planted Agent Hicks' phone in her locker. Back at the cargo hold, she moved the suitcase and the body into the elevator. Her plan was going well until a patch of turbulence struck.

The turbulence knocked the body out of the suitcase, scattering the victim's belongings everywhere. Miles Edgeworth had also fainted from the turbulence moments after Teneiro bought her suitcase for the flight. Cammy knew she didn't have any time left to clean up the mess, but she had discovered a new target to pin the crime on. She planted the victim's travel wallet on an unconscious Edgeworth to give him a motive and took a piggy bank that fell out of its shelf during the turbulence, striking Hicks' body over the head to create a fake murder weapon, then made a hasty retreat. Some time later, Edgeworth woke up, discovered the wallet and the body, and was mistakenly accused for the murder by Teneiro.

Epilogue

Cammy has been arrested and is being brought to the precinct. Teneiro thanks you and gives you a suitcase. Franziska is already booking her departure, though you intercept her before she boards.

Franziska's off to track down leads about the smuggling ring in another country, though she does state that she is working with another Interpol agent. He's very popular among Interpol and has the highest arrest rate of all investigators. She says that you might meet him someday. Perhaps you will!

A cell phone rings. The other person on the line is a man called Ernest Amano, whom you recognize. He asks you to help him rescue his son who has been kidnapped. Looks like we have another case on our hands...

THE KIDNAPPED TURNABOUT

Edgeworth has been called to help drop off the ransom to save the son of a man called Ernest Amano. With the money in his new suitcase and Gumshoe watching him from a distance, he arrives at the entrance of Gatewater Land. He is greeted by a mascot called Proto Badger. Noone knows that someone is being held ransom in this park. Suddenly, there is a call from the kidnapper. They instruct Edgeworth to move to the stadium.

At the stadium, he is instructed to go to the park's Haunted House. Broken mirrors line the walls and the usual fairground sound effects ring out constantly. A mascot lies at one end of the house's hallway. The kidnapper now instructs Edgeworth to go through the large doors. He is told to leave the money in the house's dining room and leave. But he won't be leaving very soon. Edgeworth decides to stay at the haunted house until the police arrive. Suddenly, the mascot at the back slowly rises. The figure of the Proto Badger slowly sneaks up behind Edgeworth. It holds up a sword and...

Part 3-1 - Beginning

Following the introduction where, immediately after the previous case, you were ambushed while providing ransom money to stop a kidnapping, you come to. It is raining, and someone is arguing about the ransom and police. It seems like we're now locked in in a storage room of some sort. You recall why you agreed to deliver the ransom money: to repay a debt of gratitude to Ernest Amano, the director of the powerful zaibatsu, the Amano Group, as he helped you in the past. His son, Lance, is already 20, but still got kidnapped.

Suddenly, there's another voice. A teenage girl hops down from the window. She calls herself the Great Thief Yatagarasu (although it's chronologically later, this title was also mentioned in the first case), though her real name is Kay Faraday. She unties you and you automatically **talk** to her:

- **Great Thief:** Kay insists that she is the Great Thief Yatagarasu. The title rings a bell with you...

- **Yatagarasu:** You recall knowing of a previous Yatagarasu. Kay claims that she doesn't steal ordinary things.

Kay asks for your name, after which she seems to remember something about you. Now that the introductions are settled, we can focus on escaping. The door is obviously locked, so that's not an option. Looks like the only way out is through the window that Kay came in from. Kay herself can't jump back up there, so we'll need another way.

Investigation: Isolation Room

Examine the **mascot head with sunglasses**. Kay recognizes it as part of the Bad Badger mascot costume, but why is the head the only part there? The **Bad Badger's Head** is added to the Organizer.

Now, **examine** the **small white object** on the tarp. It's your phone; you can contact the police to help you! You call Detective Gumshoe, but after a brief conversation, Gumshoe is dragged away and replaced by a new person. He introduces himself as Shi-Long Lang, an agent of Interpol. Is he the one who Franziska was talking about yesterday? He blames you for falling into the kidnapper's trap and says he can't help you escape as his team is hunting for the kidnapper. Your phone then runs out of power. Unfortunately, it seems you and Kay are on your own.

Examine the **sign on the floor**. The park is holding a Blue Badger photo rally. A prize is given to anyone who snaps a picture of all four badgers: the Blue Badger, Pink

Badger, Proto Badger and Bad Badger. There's only one of each in the park. The **Badger Photo Rally** is added to the Organizer.

Examine the **beam**. There's a small hook there and the beam leads to the window, so it might be a way to escape! Kay tries to climb it, but fails. That's not a usable escape route after all, but you get **The beam I was tied to** logic as consolation.

By now a new topic is open, so **talk** to Kay again:

- **The kidnapping:** Kay confirms that there were two kidnappers in the other room. Now we can look through the slot.

Examine the **hatch**. The **Open floor panel** is held to the wall by a hook.

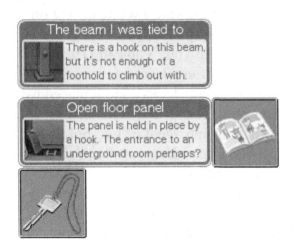

Next, **examine** the **boxes**. There's a costume of the Pink Badger in the lower right box. You aren't very familiar with the badgers so Kay gives you the **Blue Badger Bible**, which is added to the Organizer. There are eight boxes, seven of which are

32

empty, so there should be seven **Costumes** being used currently.

Now that you are in a close-up view of the boxes, **examine** the **key** at the left edge. We could probably use this **Tiny key** to open something in this room. **Examine** the **lockers**. You and Kay could escape if you can climb up the **Lockers**, but they are too high to reach. If we were to get to the top, we would need some footholds.

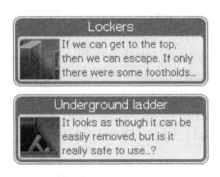

Go into Logic mode and connect **The beam I was tied to** with **Open floor panel**. The panel was held open by a hook attached to a beam. There is a beam with a hook in the room we're in, so is there an escape hatch here too? In fact, there is, just hidden under the tarp, so **examine** it. Seems like an **Underground entrance**, but it's locked, of course. Go back into Logic mode and connect **Tiny key** with **Underground entrance**. The key should unlock the panel lock, and it does! Kay dives in but falls to the ground as the ladder slips. There's machinery in the basement, but no exit that can be seen. We do know one thing, however: the **Underground ladder** is merely propped to the floor, not attached. Finally, connect **Underground ladder** with **Lockers**. We can use the ladder from the basement to climb to the top of those lockers. Freedom!

Bad Ending One: If you run out of ideas, or logic in this case, you and Kay decide to give in and wait for the police to rescue you.

Shi-Long Lang

You and Kay emerge from a building in the wild west themed area of the theme park; it seems the two of you were trapped in an underground storage room. Gumshoe comes and meets up with you, glad to see you're alright. This doesn't last long, however, as Agent Lang, the man who took your call in the storage room, arrives, accompanied by a mysterious woman called Shih-na. You and him exchange business cards. Apparently, he's the agent Franziska was talking about; he was close to the late Agent Hicks and is a little sad about his death. However, he really doesn't like prosecutors, and won't even let you investigate! Maybe you can find something out about him if you **talk** to Gumshoe:

- **Agent Lang:** Agent Lang seemed to appear out of nowhere after Gumshoe called the precinct for backup. Interpol

agents don't investigate normal domestic cases, so why is he here?
- **Next step:** Gumshoe gets into a slight argument with Kay. Nothing useful for us.

Since you still can't go anywhere, **talk** to Kay:

- **Next step:** She is still talking about stealing something.
- **One and only one:** Kay says she's after the truth. You recall that, seven years ago, there was another Yatagarasu who found evidence of corrupt dealings and made them public. The thief seemed to just infiltrate the companies and disappear, leaving a card with the mark of the three-legged raven behind. Is Kay really the next Yatagarasu...?

Ernest Amano then arrives and apologizes for you being kidnapped. You are grateful to him, as he helped introduce you to the law office and study the justice system of another country, and was a friend of your mentor, Manfred von Karma. He is in a pretty bad situation, with his son Lance still kidnapped and the ransom money stolen. You can now **talk** to him:

- **The kidnapping:** It happened out of the blue. Ernest received a phone call and heard the pleas for help from his son at the other end.
- **Lance Amano:** Lance is 21 this year, and is kind and attractive. Ernest also has a butler called Oliver Deacon, though he's nowhere to be seen. He's very close with Lance, so he might know who would want to kidnap him.

- **Oliver Deacon:** Deacon was a very loyal butler, though Ernest hasn't heard from him after his recent leave. His relatives and friends haven't seen him, either. Suspicious...

Well, you can't just idle around here forever. Time to begin your investigation, whether the Interpol agent lets you or not!

Bad Ending Two: If you run out of logic during this investigation, Lang forces you to leave. Despite your protests, Lang tells you to go back to the courtroom.

Investigation: Wild, Wild West Area

Gumshoe is dragged away by the precinct detectives to work for Lang, so we only have Kay as an assistant. You can't leave this area, so you should see what you can learn about around here. Try to **talk** to the Blue Badger mascot. Initially, he just dances around, though Kay pulls off the mascot's head revealing... Mike Meekins? You remember him as a witness from one of your past cases.

- **Mike Meekins:** Meekins is not currently a police officer, though he still wishes to become a detective.
- **Blue Badger:** Meekins was ordered by Agent Lang to disguise himself as the Blue Badger to catch the kidnappers.
- **Any clues?:** Meekins had been standing here for an hour around the time you woke up. He could've seen the kidnappers escape! He claims he didn't see anything, however.

Meekins says that he only saw a Blue Badger when he was standing here. That's contradictory with something we already know, though. **Present** the **Badger Photo Rally**. There can only be one of each badger in the park at any time, and Meekins is already wearing the Blue Badger outfit! If what Meekins said was true, there must have been **A 2nd Blue Badger** walking around in the park, but why?

Examine the **area around the pipe**. There are a bunch of footprints around here, though we don't know which sets belong to the kidnappers. You get the **What kind of shoes?** logic.

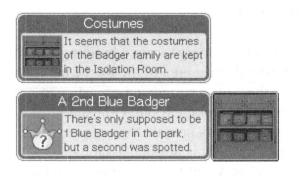

Go into Logic mode and connect **Costumes** with **A 2nd Blue Badger**. Since there are seven costumes in use currently, the kidnappers must have been disguised as them! You get the **Costumed escape** logic. The stolen costumes are that of a Blue Badger, a Proto Badger and a Bad Badger. The kidnappers could still be wandering around in the park wearing those outfits. The **Stolen Costumes** are added to the Organizer. Now connect **What kind of shoes?** with **Costumed escape**. Since the kidnappers were disguised as badgers, you should follow the costume's paw prints.

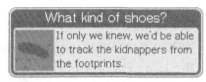

What kind of shoes?
If only we knew, we'd be able to track the kidnappers from the footprints.

Costumed escape
The identity of the second Blue Badger was probably the kidnapper in disguise.

Examine the **area where you found the footprints** again. There are two sets, one leading to the west and on to the wooden floor and one headed east to where Meekins is standing. He's not the kidnapper, so maybe one of them walked to the garage. It is currently closed, so **examine** it to open it. Inside there is... a dead body! Ernest recognizes him as Oliver Deacon, his butler. The set of footprints ended here, so is Deacon a kidnapper? You get the **Victim was kidnapper?** logic. Looks like he died from a bullet wound. The **Preliminary Findings** are added to the Organizer.

Agent Lang could be here any minute, so you'd better find out as much as you can before he arrives. **Examine** the **victim's wound**. It looks like he was shot in the abdomen and the shoulder, but you determine that he wasn't shot twice, but rather, a single bullet traveled through his abdomen to his shoulder. For a bullet that penetrated the whole way, there is very little blood on the crime scene...
The **Preliminary Findings** are updated in the Organizer. Next, **examine** the **pendant**. There's a name on the back of it: Colin

Devorae. But that isn't the victim's name... **Deduce** the **pendant** and **present** the **Preliminary Findings**. The victim's name is Oliver Deacon, not Colin Devorae. **Mr. Deacon's Pendant** is added to your Organizer. With that, our investigation is complete!

Bad Ending Three: If you run out of logic here, Lang disrupts the investigation and tells you to go back to the courtroom.

Meekins's Arrest

A woman then walks into the area. She introduces herself as Lauren Paups, the girlfriend of Lance. She came here after she heard about the kidnapping.

Agent Lang returns and sees the crime scene. He detains Meekins as a suspect right away. That's a bit hasty, but Lang insists that it's the way he stops crime. His line of logic is faulty, and you must prove Meekins' innocence.

Lang's Argument: Shi-Long Lang's Logic

1. I've seen a lot of bodies like this one being carted off in my time.
2. I can say he was shot in a single glance, but even you figured that much out, right?
3. With your current gun laws, it's not exactly easy to get your hands on a gun.
4. Not unless you're a member of law

35

enforcement like Officer Meekins, isn't that right?

Lang says that he follows the "detainment philosophy" developed by Zheng Faian philosopher Lang Zi thousands of years ago, which is still used by Zheng Fa's police today. Let's put that philosophy to the test.

Rebuttal: Shi-Long Lang's Logic

Press the fourth statement. Meekins's gun is the only one that has been fired, but he claims he lost his gun! That's not good. You get a new statement:

- Officer Meekins ambushed the victim in this garage and killed him here with his gun!

Present the Preliminary Findings at this new statement. There is simply too little blood at the crime scene, so this garage might not be the crime scene at all. Lang asks us another question: why was Officer Meekins standing right outside the location of the victim's body all this time? Meekins claims he simply took a walk, but it's obvious he's hiding something.

Meekins' Testimony: Meekins's Testimony

1. It's true, sir! I wasn't assigned to this area, sir!
2. I was told to check every square inch of the main gate area, sir!

3. I also went looking for the kidnappers while selling dreams in the Blue Badgermobile, sir!
4. But! I got completely caught up in my role, selling dreams to the children! SIR!
5. Before I knew it, I found myself in this area, sir!

You ask about the Blue Badgermobile, and Meekins explains that it's a mobile souvenir shop. The Blue Badgermobile is added to the Organizer.

Rebuttal: Meekins's Testimony

Present the Blue Badgermobile at the third statement. The Blue Badgermobile is parked in the garage, so he couldn't have been using it. Meekins claims that he lost it, so he went back to find it in the garage, meeting you there. Lang doesn't believe the story at all and arrests Meekins regardless. There is no way you can stop him since he is the one who calls the shots!

Bad Ending Four: If you can't win this argument once you run out of logic, Lang arrests Meekins on the spot. Poor Meekins.

Part 3-2 - Middle 1

Even though you're chased out, you insist on finding the true murderer. The first order of business is to find the real crime scene. Gumshoe arrives and informs you about a witness at the stadium. There's no one here... except Ema Skye, who was the defendant in one of your past cases. She's now studying abroad to become a forensic scientist, so she's only in the country for spring break. **Talk** to her:

- **Ema Skye:** She mentions that she has a kit that lets her spray for footprints. That could be useful.
- **The witness:** She didn't witness anything, though she did say that Gumshoe had called her there.

Examine the Pink Badgermobile parked nearby. The Pink Badger runs to the stadium. There's nothing to do but to talk to her. It turns out that she is none other than Wendy Oldbag, a character from the first and second games! Watch out for her - she loves talking but loves you more!

- **Wendy Oldbag:** Nothing useful to you. If you want to know more, the first two games will allow you to know her better.
- **The witness:** Oldbag says she did see the murder!

This is a big lead! You ask her to testify about what she saw.

Oldbag's Testimony: What Oldbag Witnessed

1. I came to this stadium to take a short break.

2. As I was resting, I happened to glance over and I saw two men facing each other in the area.
3. Suddenly, there was a loud gunshot, and the person who was shot fell to the ground.
4. It was a very terrifying experience, let me tell you!

Rebuttal: What Oldbag Witnessed

Press every statement. Oldbag doesn't remember any of the men's features because she thought they were too uninteresting. Seems like a dead end... or is it? Kay now introduces Little Thief, a new gadget that she claims is her secret weapon. This is a projection device that can simulate any situation! This could show any errors in Oldbag's testimony. After inputting some information into the device, she projects a recreation image over the whole area.

Investigation: Stadium Re-creation

An investigation in a re-creation is the same as normal; just walk up to things and examine them. Examine the **victim's body**. You say that this scene contradicts the facts of the murder. Present **Mr. Deacon's Murder Notes**. There's no blood on the floor, but Oldbag isn't someone who would lie to you, so... **Why is there no blood?**

Now go into Logic Mode and connect **Victim was kidnapper?** with **Why is there no blood?**. If the victim was a kidnapper and was shot while wearing a costume, it can explain why there isn't any blood on the crime scene. If only you could prove that he was wearing a costume... You need to find footprints, but you can't see any. Fortunately, there's one person here who could help you out with that. **Talk** to Ema:

- **Footprint analysis:** She agrees to help you find footprints using her science kit.

After some spraying, Ema detects footprints. They aren't visible to the naked eye, though they are when wearing Ema's special glasses. The victim was wearing a costume at the time he died. **Victim's Costume** is added to your Organizer. Kay updates her re-creation with the footprints, and that marks the completion of your investigation! You note that there's something that you're suspicious of, and ask to hear Oldbag's testimony again.

Oldbag's Testimony: What Oldbag Witnessed

1. I came to this stadium to take a short break.
2. As I was resting, I happened to glance over and I saw two men facing each other in the area.
3. Suddenly, there was a loud gunshot, and the person who was shot fell to the ground.
4. It was a very terrifying experience, let me tell you!

Rebuttal: What Oldbag Witnessed

Present the **Victim's Costume** at **statement 2**. How did she know that the victim and the killer were men if they were wearing costumes? And why didn't she mention the costumes in her testimony? Oldbag says she made the mistake as she witnessed it from the second tier seats of the stadium. She says she couldn't see what they looked like because they were **In the shadow of the stage**. Now you can resume your investigation.

Investigation: Stadium Re-creation

First, examine the stage. It looks like the **Stage was packed up** since you last saw it. Now go into Logic Mode and connect **Stage was packed up** with **In the shadow of the stage**. If Oldbag's testimony was true, the murder must have happened before the stage was broken down. Kay updates her re-creation and... aha! A blatant contradiction! Unless the killer could move through solid metal, he couldn't have been standing there. Oldbag recalls that she did see the killer standing on the stage when they shot the victim. Kay updates the re-creation again. There's something not right about this scene, but your investigation is cut short as Agent Lang arrives. He instructs his men to recreate the scene in reality and still asserts that Officer Meekins was the killer.

Lang's Argument: Agent Lang's Logic

1. This is the real scene of the crime.
2. Officer Meekins lay in wait for the victim on top of the stage.
3. And when the victim finally showed, he shot him from on high!
4. That's the truth your little re-creation showed.

Rebuttal: Agent Lang's Logic

Present Mr. Deacon's Murder Notes on the **third statement**. The bullet entered his body in the abdomen and exited through the shoulder. The bullet couldn't have traveled like that if the killer was standing on the stage! There is one parameter that was flawed in the virtual re-creation, and that was **The killer's and victim's locations**. The victim was the one standing on top of the stage! As the footprints now lead to where the killer is standing, it can be safe to assume that the killer was also wearing a badger costume. That means that the murderer could have been another kidnapper. Agent Lang still doesn't accept Officer Meekins' innocence, though.

Lang's Argument: Another Bit of Proof

1. I ask that you take another good look at the tire marks over there.
2. The three marks are indicative of the Blue Badgermobile.

3. That story Officer Meekins told about that shop on wheels getting stolen was just a lie.
4. He drove the Blue Badgermobile here and committed the murder.
5. Then, he used the car to move the body to the garage in the Wild, Wild West Area.

Rebuttal: Another Bit of Proof

Present the **Blue Badgermobile** on the **second statement**. The Blue Badgermobile could not have left the marks behind the stadium. Present the **Blue Badgermobile's tires** as proof. The tires don't have any mud on them! The Pink Badgermobile and Proto Badgermobile could've made those marks, but since Oldbag probably isn't related to the case, that leaves the Proto Badgermobile as the one responsible for leaving those marks. Suddenly, a man walks near the stadium calling for help before collapsing. It's Lance, the kidnapped man! He says he was held at the Wild, Wild West Area and escaped through the underground floor. He also recalls that the kidnappers were wearing costumes when they escaped and that one of them was a woman. Agent Lang once again chases us off the crime scene and keeps Oldbag and Ema for questioning.

Bad Ending Five: If you run out of logic here, Lang accuses you of interfering with the case. Also, he orders his men to arrest Meekins of his crime.

Part 3-3 - Middle 2

Once again, you're kicked out of the investigation. Ernest and Paups meet up with you, having learned that Lance is safe. **Talk** to Ernest first:

- **Lance Amano:** Ernest has a letter to pass to his son after the police have finished questioning him. What kind of letter...?
- **Letter:** It appears that Lance has received yet another love letter. Well, not quite; it's from Viola of Tender Lender, both names which should be familiar to players of Trials and Tribulations. The **Love Letter** is added to your Organizer.

Now **talk** to Paups:

- **Lance Amano:** Paups is so close to Lance because her father used to work for Ernest. He flew around the world on an airplane called Pegasus but disappeared ten years ago while flying it.
- **About the case:** Paups claims she knew about the kidnapping from her intuition.

The killer must be another kidnapper, so there should be one place where we can gather more clues, which is the **Kidnapper's Hideout**. Agent Lang should be done investigating the area, so we should be able to enter the hideout. The officer guarding it lets us in and gives us a

document about the victim. The victim's real name wasn't Oliver Deacon! He was actually Colin Devorae and was convicted of a crime ten years ago, having broken out of jail since. The **Colin Devorae Dossier** is added to your Organizer. The officer says that the door had to be broken down by about ten officers, which means Agent Lang must have already done his investigation here, though there might be some clues left.

Investigation: Kidnapper's Hideout

First, examine the **door** that you came in through. You enter a close-up scene. Examine the **door handle**. The handle is in a bad state thanks to the previous break-in, but the door lock is somehow undamaged. You get **The door leading outside** logic. Next, examine the **grey objects** lying on the floor. It appears to be a **Broken prop sword**, but why is it broken in the first place?

Examine the **blue bin** at the bottom. It's where the old badger costumes are thrown away. You note that they are disposed of in pieces. You get the **Costume pieces** logic.

Examine the **table** for another close-up scene. Examine the **cups** to get the **3 cups** logic. Then, examine the three chairs to get the **Folding chairs** logic.

Now go into Logic Mode. First, connect **The door leading outside** with **Broken prop sword**. The sword must've been used to jam the unlocked door, resulting in the handle being broken but not the lock itself. The **Broken Prop Sword** is added to your Organizer. Next, connect **Folding chairs** with **3 cups**. Three cups used, three folding chairs, and three costumes stolen would mean three kidnappers, though Lance only saw two. Suddenly, a Proto Badger head pops out from the hatch! He says that this underground passage is used by staff members and other badgers. After going into the Isolation Room, he says that the Bad Badger costume is gone, even though he was told that only three costumes were stolen.

Talk to the **Proto Badger**. (If you pay attention to how he speaks, you may notice he's actually the hotel bellboy from the first game in disguise!) Both costumes ought to be in the Isolation Room normally because the Bad Badger only appears during a certain event at a set time where he appears to fight the other badgers and get apprehended. That means that four costumes were stolen, but not necessarily

41

four kidnappers stole it. There's one thing that shows the fourth kidnapper doesn't exist. **Present** the **Pink Badger costume**. The kidnappers stole a second Bad Badger costume instead of simply stealing the Pink Badger costume, but why? You get the **Unaccounted for Bad Badger** logic.

Go into Logic Mode and connect the **Costume pieces** with **Unaccounted for Bad Badger**. The second Bad Badger costume is right in the bin, though it lacks the head. You go into a close-up view of the costume. First, examine the **right hand**. A piece of cloth is ripped off. Deduce the **right hand** and present the **Blue Badger Bible**. The costume is also missing its gun. The Proto Badger explains that the gun is just a model but can fire blanks. The **Missing Model Gun** is added to your Organizer. And with that, your investigation is complete!

Bad Ending Six: If you lose your logic here or at the stadium, Lang arrests Meekins despite your protests.

A new discovery!

Upon exiting the hideout, Gumshoe runs up to you. He informs you that a Blue Badger costume has been found at the entrance. If you hurry, you could get there before Agent Lang does!

Part 3-4 - End 1

It turns out that the spare Blue Badger costume was hidden in some tall grass before it was discovered. Since Agent Lang has yet to arrive, you can investigate the costume. **Examine** the **silver object** in its neck hole. It looks similar to the victim's pendant, but before you can figure anything out, Agent Lang interrupts you. He says that it's a piece of decisive evidence, as it has the name "Lauren" engraved in the back. **Ms. Paups's Pendant** is added to your Organizer. That means that Lauren Paups is one of the kidnappers, which she confesses to. Agent Lang now shifts his suspicion of the murderer to Paups, as his team found Officer Meekins' gun that didn't show signs of having been fired. Paups confesses to this too! This case can't be that simple, so she must be hiding something. You request that she give a testimony.

Paups' Testimony: Ms. Paups's Confession

1. The one who came up with the kidnapping plan was the butler, Mr. Deacon.
2. We knew that we could get rich by holding Lance hostage.
3. Mr. Amano would pay anything to get his son back, after all.
4. Everything was going according to plan, but as soon as we got the money...
5. ...Mr. Deacon turned on me, and tried to kill me!

Rebuttal: Ms. Paups's Confession

Press her **fifth statement**, and **raise an objection** when prompted. Paups says that Deacon probably planned to kill her from the very beginning, though he couldn't have. **Raise an objection** and **present Ms. Paups's Pendant**, then **present Mr. Deacon's Pendant**. They have a similar color and are made of the same material, so they could be one pendant. Connecting them makes a Pegasus pendant. Now, for extra proof, **present** the **Colin Devorae Dossier**. Oliver Deacon was just an alias of the victim, used to avoid capture after he broke out of jail, but there's one thing that holds special interest. **Present** the words **sole daughter**. Colin Devorae is Lauren Paups' father, so surely he couldn't have planned to turn on his own daughter? Lang thinks there's another possibility why Devorae turned on Lauren.

Lang's Argument: Another Possibility

1. I'll grant you that the two of them are father and daughter.
2. But, isn't it possible that they both knew that fact?
3. It was no coincidence that the reunited pair became involved in the house of Amano.
4. And the two of them made good use of their meetings to plan this little kidnapping.
5. Wouldn't you say my scenario is perfectly probable as well?

Rebuttal: Another Possibility

Present the **Stolen Costumes** at the **fourth statement**. Four costumes were stolen by the kidnappers, though one is found at the kidnapper's hideout. That means there must have been a third kidnapper. The third kidnapper could be the mastermind of the kidnapping. When asked who he is, **present Lance Amano's profile**. Lance doesn't seem to recall a third kidnapper, so he could be simply faking the kidnapping. Agent Lang and Lance himself say that Lance wouldn't have seen all the kidnappers while he was kidnapped. Lance tries to recall his kidnapping.

Lance's Testimony: Lance's Testimony

1. I was kidnapped yesterday morning.
2. They had me shut in that room, blindfolded, the entire time.
3. But the kidnappers suddenly disappeared around the time I heard rain falling outside.
4. My hands were cuffed, but it was a stroke of luck that they left me alone.
5. I made my escape and ran away from that room as fast as I could.

Rebuttal: Lance's Testimony

Press the **fifth statement** to get a new piece of testimony about Lance's escape.

- The door leading outside was locked

tight, so I had to use the underground passageway.

Present the **Broken Prop Sword** on this new statement. The door itself was unlocked - only the sword was jamming the door up until Agent Lang's men broke into it. Even if his hands were cuffed, Lance could easily have removed the sword. Lance must have locked himself in to pretend he was being held captive, but because he didn't have the key to the door, he had to use the prop sword. Agent Lang says that Lance doesn't have a motive to fake a kidnapping, but he does! **Present** the **Love Letter**. This love letter isn't a love letter at all, but a collection bill from a loan company. Lance was in quite a debt, so he had to fake his own kidnapping to get the money to repay it.

Lance confesses that he kidnapped himself, though he was later betrayed by Devorae. The victim attacked Lance when he was alone, though Lance managed to subdue him. Then, he and Paups escaped by wearing the costumes and getting away separately. Paups wore the Blue Badger costume and escaped first, but Lance was attacked again by Devorae. He then put on a Bad Badger costume and took the money. Lance contacted Paups and warned her about the victim. Paups still thinks that she killed her own father.

Paups' Testimony: Chain of Events

1. That man was not my father! I mean... Because... at the stadium...

2. There was a Bad Badger pulling the suitcase with the $1 million in it.
3. But that Badger pointed his gun at me, aiming to shoot me dead!
4. That's why I... I used the gun I got from Lance...!
5. There was a gunshot, the other person crumpled to the ground, and I ran, scared for my life.

Rebuttal: Chain of Events

Press statement three. You get a revised piece of testimony.

• But that Badger pointed the gun in his left hand at me, aiming to shoot me dead!

Present the **Colin Devorae Dossier** on this new statement. The victim was right-handed, so the person that aimed at her couldn't have been her own father! Agent Lang then says that the Bad Badger had a model gun in his right hand, so the victim could only have used his left hand to hold the real gun. If that's the case, then the Bad Badger must've been carrying the gun in his left hand and the suitcase with his right hand. There's an obvious contradiction here, so the only way to explain it is that **Both are correct**. There was a way for the Bad Badger to use both hands freely. **Present** the **Bad Badger's Head**. The head of the costume could have easily been matched with the body of another costume. Which one? **Present** the **Proto Badger**. The Pink Badger's body is a different color and Paups was already

44

wearing the Blue Badger costume at the time, so the only possibility is that the person she killed was wearing a Proto Badger body.

Paups says that Lance was wearing the Proto Badger costume. Lance was only pretending to be the victim so that Paups would have thought that she killed the victim. There is only one reason Lance would want to do that, and that's because he was the murderer! Lance reveals that he is indeed left-handed, which matches Paups' testimony. Agent Lang says that Lance must know that the bullet could have passed right through his costume and killed him, and he probably did, so he did something to prevent him from being killed. **Present** the **Missing Model Gun**. The model gun has been ripped off of the disposed-of Bad Badger costume, and it can fire blanks. Paups threw the gun into the sea, so there's no way to prove our case. We also don't know where the murder really took place. The murder must have taken place at an earlier time.

Paups says that she witnessed the victim in a restrained state, so he couldn't have been killed any earlier. Or could he?

Paups' Testimony: What Ms. Paups Saw

1. I came back to the hideout long after the other two.
2. By that time, Lance had already subdued and restrained Mr. Deacon.
3. He had tied Mr. Deacon securely to the beam in the room next door.

4. After that, the two of us put on our costumes and made our escape.

Rebuttal: What Ms. Paups Saw

Press statement three. You get a new piece of testimony.

- The captive had a Bad Badger's head on, so I'm absolutely sure it was Mr. Deacon.

Press this new statement and **raise an objection**. **Present** the **Bad Badger's Head** and, when asked to choose who it could have been instead, select **Miles Edgeworth**. The kidnappers abducted you to make you look like the victim! If you were mistaken for the victim by Paups, that means the victim had already died by then. Lance then let Paups escape first before removing the Bad Badger head and staging the murder. However, since Paups never actually checked who the captive was, she couldn't verify that you were there either!

Bad Ending Six: If your logic runs out here, Lang arrests Paups, telling you that your logic needs work. Paups says she'll pay for her actions.

Another costume

Out of nowhere, Ernest arrives to make up for his son's actions by presenting a new piece of evidence. It's the missing Bad Badger costume! Ernest says that he fished the costume and the gun from the sea, and explains that he has gotten permission from the Chief of Police to do as he pleases. He had it privately examined by a group of forensics experts, who confirmed that the blood was the victim's and the fingerprints on the gun belonged to Paups.

Examine the **neck hole** of the head. There are pieces of a mirror in it, but why?
The **Mirror Fragments** are added to your Organizer. Then, **examine** the **gun** on the badger's abdomen to add the **Revolver** to your Organizer.
Finally, **examine** the **bullet hole**. The hole has burnt marks around it, which means that the victim was shot point-blank.
The **Victim's Costume** is updated in your Organizer. It's up to Lance to tell us his version of events again.

Bad Ending Seven: If you run out of logic after Ernest finds the missing costume, Lance decides that you are wasting everyone's time. Ernest decides to let the court go through its process, leading to Lance being acquitted of charges due to a lack of evidence.

Lance's Testimony: Decisive Evidence

1. Make no mistake. There are fingerprints on that murderous gun.
2. And they proved that it was Lolli who killed Oliver.
3. But Oliver was also after Lolli's life.
4. So Mr. Edgeworth, even you must see that Lolli was only acting in self-defense.

Rebuttal: Decisive Evidence

Press Lance's **first statement** and **Raise an objection**. Paups' prints couldn't have been on the gun. **Present** either the **Stolen Costumes**, the **Bad Badger's Head**, or the **Blue Badger Bible**. Paups was wearing a costume while she was at the stadium, so how could she have left prints? Her fingerprints could have been left when she touched it when the other kidnappers went to collect the ransom money. We also have proof that the whole murder is, in fact, set up. **Present** the **Victim's Costume** and then the **bullet hole**. If the victim was shot from below the stage, there shouldn't have been any burn marks!

Agent Lang now challenges you to give the true crime scene. The only place Lance and the victim were alone was when they went to collect the ransom. **Present** the **Haunted House**, then **present** the **Mirror Fragments**. The fragments were found in the costume, and the only place they could have come from was the Haunted House. Agent Lang states that there is another broken mirror at the hideout, and although it is much less likely for the fragments to get into the costume, we can't prove that the fragments came from the Haunted House!

If you can prove the murder happened at the Haunted House, you can prove Lance's guilt! Unfortunately, Ernest states that he bought the deed to the Haunted House while you were arguing, and denies you from investigating it. That's a big problem for your case...

Part 3-5 - End 2

Looks like all hope is lost. Ernest has denied you permission to investigate the Haunted House. Lauren will be arrested while Lance will get away with murder. The truth will be lost to us all. It's the end... or is it? Kay reminds you that she still has Little Thief! That way, you can recreate the scene at the Haunted House based on its blueprints.

The first thing you should recreate is the moment you were ambushed. When you were dropping off the ransom, you saw a badger mannequin lying at the other end of the corridor. Once you turned your back, you were struck from behind. Looking at a map, as the hallway is a dead end, that can only mean that the assailant was waiting to attack you at **point B**! The costumed attacker lay in wait disguised as an unsuspicious prop at the end of the corridor, then ambushed you as you turned to leave. Lance claims that he never went into the Haunted House, just waited outside, so that means that the victim, who was wearing the Bad Badger costume, is your attacker. As the Bad Badger had a model gun attached to its right hand, the weapon must have been held in the left hand.

Investigation: Haunted House Re-creation

First, examine the **mirrors**. There's a lot of mirrors in here, and some of them are already broken, so it isn't surprising that there were some **Mirror shards** found in the victim's costume. Kay notes that the mirror shards here, however, are thicker and have some sort of design at the back.

The **Mirror Fragments** are updated in your Organizer.

Now examine the **Bad Badger** behind you. You don't know what weapon was used to hit you, though you remember getting hit on the right side of your head. There could be a weapon in the hallway that the assailant could have used to knock you out. Present the **Broken Prop Sword**. The attacker could have used it to attack you, then took it to the hideout to hide the evidence, which is why it was found there. You can run a test to determine whether it was used to attack you. The attacker couldn't have left any prints as he was a costumed kidnapper, so you should **Test with Luminol**. Your wound bled slightly after you were struck, so there could be some blood on the sword. After testing, there is a small patch of blood on the left side. The **Broken Prop Sword** is updated in your Organizer. The re-creation is also updated to include the sword.

There's something wrong about this scene, though. Going into a close-up, deduce the **sword** and present the **Broken Prop Sword**. If the sword was held in the left hand, it would hit on the left side, so the bloodied right side could only have resulted from a right-handed swing. Kay changes the re-creation to reflect this new fact, but we know there will be another contradiction. Present the **Missing Model Gun** or the **Blue Badger Bible**. There is already a model gun attached to the Bad Badger's right hand, so the Bad Badger couldn't have been the attacker. This leaves Lance as the culprit, and he confesses to it.

Even though he's left-handed, he used his right hand on purpose to pin it on Devorae.

Now the re-creation is updated once again, with the Proto Badger as the attacker, which matches the opening cinematic of this case quite well. However, Agent Lang interrupts us before we can investigate. He reveals that the Haunted House had a trick called the "disappearing badger". A Blue Badger doll was placed at that very end of the corridor as the disappearing badger, so the attacker couldn't have been hiding there! The **Gatewater Land Pamphlet** is updated in your Organizer. The re-creation is also updated once again. There is something blatantly wrong about the scene, as the Blue Badger simply turns into a Proto Badger.

Examine the **Blue Badger doll** at the end of the hallway. There's something peculiar about it. Deduce the **belt** and present the **Blue Badger Bible** or **Badger Photo Rally**. The belt seems to be mirrored from the actual Blue Badger costume, but Kay says that it was an exact re-creation of the picture in the pamphlet. Why is the **Blue Badger in reverse**?

Go into Logic Mode and connect the **Mirror shards** with **Blue Badger in reverse**. The Blue Badger doll you saw was actually a mirrored image. The corridor is not actually straight - it forms an L-shape at the end of the hallway, where the real doll lies. It is reflected by the mirror at the bend of the hallway. As the house is dark, the trick is concealed perfectly. There could be one reason why the park built the house in this way. Present the **Gatewater Land Pamphlet**. The disappearing badger is one of the seven wonders of the attraction, but you had no trouble seeing the badger. There is a trick that the someone could have used to make the doll disappear, and that is to **Move the mirror-wall**. When the badger doll is visible, the mirror is at its normal location. When the doll disappears, the mirror wall simply moves to close the end with the badger doll, revealing an empty corridor behind it. That is why the mirror fragments had a pattern behind them, to blend in with the wall!

48

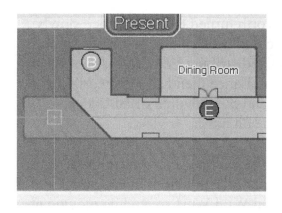

It also presents a new hiding place for the attacker. Present the **corridor behind the mirror**. The assailant only had to wait behind the mirror where you couldn't see him, then strike by moving the mirror away. However, since we have some of the mirror fragments, the mirror wall must be broken in the real Haunted House. As they were found in the victim's costume, it means the victim was there when the mirror broke. You also recall the sound of glass breaking as soon as the phone call with one of the kidnappers ended.

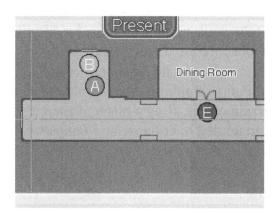

Kay recreates the scene with the mirror wall. Before you entered the dining room, the kidnappers were hiding behind the mirror wall. After you entered the dining room, the wall broke and the kidnapper's hideout was revealed. The kidnapper then

had to hide at the end of the hallway with the doll. There is another contradiction here. Present the **empty straight corridor**. When you went out of the dining room, you still saw a badger at the end of the corridor, when there shouldn't be anything there. Present the **Victim's Costume** or **Mr. Deacon's Murder Notes**. That badger could be the dead body of the victim! You didn't hear the gunshot itself because there were a bunch of other sound effects playing in the house at the time.

With the evidence stacking up against him, Lance finally breaks down and confesses to the murder.

What really happened

Ten years ago, the Amano Group was revealed to have an internal smuggling ring which caused the KG-8 incident. The group's secretary, Colin Devorae, was arrested as the ringleader, but some agents suspected that it was company head Ernest Amano pinning the crime on him. Devorae soon broke out of jail, bringing with him a guard's gun. He took on the alias of "Oliver Deacon" and went back to his former employer to seek hiding. Ernest Amano promised to hide him as long as he remained silent about the true ringleader.

Ernest's son, Lance Amano, knew about "Deacon" being the missing father of his girlfriend Lauren Paups, so he used Paups as a hostage to force Deacon to cooperate in his staged kidnapping so he could pay back his $1 million of debt. As Deacon was still a felon, he couldn't reveal his identity to his daughter. All three of them staged the kidnapping together, pretending to hold Lance hostage in Gatewater Land. Edgeworth, as the protégé of Amano's close friend Manfred von Karma, was asked by Amano to drop the ransom that would save his son.

After arriving, Edgeworth was requested by one of the kidnappers to drop the ransom money at the Haunted House. The kidnappers had already made their way there after stealing the park's badger costumes, with Lance as the Proto Badger and Deacon as the Bad Badger. They hid behind the mirror wall that was used to create an illusion as part of the attraction. As Edgeworth was dropping off the ransom in the dining room, Deacon turned on Lance to make him leave his daughter out of the crime. Lance was straddled to the ground but managed to take Deacon's gun and fire a lethal shot that went straight through his body and broke the mirror wall behind them.

Having accidentally committed murder, Lance needed to pin the crime on someone else. First, he used Devorae's dead body to create the illusion that the badger Edgeworth saw was still there while he hid in a separate corridor hidden from view. As

50

Edgeworth turned to leave, Lance slowly sneaked up behind him, grabbing a prop sword and striking Edgeworth, knocking him out. Lance then had Edgeworth tied to a pole and put Devorae's Bad Badger costume on him.

Lance moved the dead body with the Proto Badgermobile and hid it in the garage in the Wild Wild West area while moving an unconscious Edgeworth to the Isolation Room. He had Paups look at Edgeworth and made her believe that he was Devorae to fake the time of the murder. He also tore off a model gun from another Bad Badger costume to give to Paups to defend herself.

Lance made Paups escape early in a Blue Badger costume before taking the badger head off of Edgeworth for himself. He lied to her that Devorae had escaped and put on the Bad Badger head on. He jammed the door with the prop sword he attacked Edgeworth with and escaped through the underground tunnels. He then pretended to be Devorae walking on the stage, having its shadow obscure the details of his costume. Once he saw Paups, he aimed at her with his gun. Paups, thinking that Devorae was going to shoot her, fired a blank at Lance. Lance pretended to collapse and Paups ran away in fright.

Epilogue

Agent Lang now calls for the arrest of Lance... and his father! He reveals that he came to the country to investigate Ernest Amano, whose company scandal, an internal smuggling ring discovered ten years ago, triggered the "KG-8 incident".

The mastermind that was arrested was Colin Devorae, the victim! Lang suspects that Ernest was the real ringleader but placed the blame on Devorae, so after Devorae escaped from prison, he chose to hide him from the police in exchange for his silence about the true ringleader. However, he is interrupted by none other than Jacques Portsman, the prosecutor for the case, with his top detective, Buddy Faith.

The two suspects are still arrested, and Lang reveals that he suspected that you were the corrupt prosecutor that worked for Ernest. After leaving, his assistant Shih-na reveals that Agent Lang belonged to the House of Lang in Zheng Fa. They were revered and held high positions among the police force there. However, a prosecutor once tampered with the evidence a Lang detective found, ruining their credibility and honor, which is why Agent Lang hates prosecutors and the court system. Portsman also leaves with his partner as you plan to head back to your office, leading to the first case of the game.

After all that has happened, Kay is still annoyed that neither you nor Gumshoe remember her. What does that mean? She presents a white cloth which jogs both of your memories. Just when you think we're done with flashbacks, we get one more, this time taking us back seven years to the time you first met Gumshoe and Kay.

TURNABOUT REMINISCENCE

Part 4-1 - Beginning

First Case

Being set seven years ago, you note that this case is your first assignment, to replace the prosecutor who was accused by the defendant of being the Yatagarasu. Ace Attorney veterans will remember that Edgeworth's actual first case was set nearly six months later, against another defense attorney and about a different murder, so something must have happened during this case.

A man enters, who fans of the first game will recognize as Edgeworth's mentor and Franziska's father, Manfred von Karma. He demands perfection from you to land the defendant in prison. Looks like this could be the first time you play the role of a prosecutor in an Ace Attorney game! **Talk** to Manfred. He says that the defendant claimed that the prosecutor, Byrne Faraday, instructed him to commit murder. We have a whole hour of recess to prepare for the case.

- **Today's trial:** A murder was committed on September 8th in front of the Cohdopian Embassy. The victim is Mr. Deid Mann, a staff member at the embassy. The defendant is Mr. Mack Rell, who was arrested as he possessed the murder weapon and was caught on the embassy's security camera. The Yatagarasu had also successfully infiltrated the Cohdopian Embassy around this time. At first, the defendant claimed to be the Yatagarasu but didn't kill anyone. Once Prosecutor Faraday presented the security footage where the defendant shot the victim, he admitted to the murder but claimed that the prosecutor is really the Yatagarasu and instructed him to do it. Von Karma also mentions that this case is has been considered by some to be the "second

KG-8 incident".

- **"2nd KG-8 incident"**: Von Karma gives us a newspaper dated three years back. The **KG-8 Incident Overview** is added to your Organizer. The Amano Group was involved in a smuggling ring, and the ringleader, Colin Devorae, was arrested. A woman named Cece Yew was the sole witness of the ring but was killed before she could provide any testimony. The killer was suspected to be a Cohdopian Embassy staff member named Manny Coachen, who was found not guilty due to insufficient evidence. The prosecutor for that case was also Byrne Faraday. The victim this time is also a witness of the smuggling organization and was also murdered before he could testify.
- **Yatagarasu:** The Yatagarasu stole something from the Cohdopian Embassy and sent it to the police. That was actually the first time the Yatagarasu incriminated itself by leaving evidence behind. Manfred suggests we ask Faraday about the Yatagarasu, as he is in charge of the

case as well.

Suddenly, a young girl enters the lobby and asks you to exchange her pile of coins for a dollar. She does seem a bit familiar, but now's not the time to think about it. The prosecutor substitution paperwork has been completed and the trial is just about to start.

Empty courthouse

There is nobody in the courtroom except for the prosecution and the bailiff - not even the defense attorney is here. The Judge now arrives, saying that he heard a popper go off during the recess. Faraday didn't even transfer his evidence to us, so how are we supposed to start the trial?

Then, none other than Detective Gumshoe barges in, saying that both the defendant and the previous prosecutor have been found dead in Defendant Lobby No. 2!

Two deaths in one

Outside the door to the defendant's lobby, a tall detective blocks our path. He denies us entry to the crime scene. The defense attorney is also here, and Gumshoe soon catches up to us. We'd better start asking around to find out what happened. **Talk** to the detective. He introduces himself as Detective Tyrell Badd. Faraday requested him to testify about the case, which is why he was already near the crime scene when you arrived.

- **Crime scene:** The prosecutor was stabbed to death holding a gun in his hand, while the defendant was shot to death with a bloodied knife in his hand. Detective Gumshoe was guarding the lobby entrance the whole time and saw no one enter, which means that the two victims killed each other!

- **Trial witness:** Badd was called as a witness because he worked on the Yatagarasu's case, so he can identify if Faraday has the Yatagarasu's characteristics.

Now **talk** to the defense attorney. Her name is Calisto Yew, and she tends to break out with laughter a lot.

- **Crime scene:** She doesn't know anything about the murder, and she's only there after hearing the news that Faraday was murdered.

Finally, **talk** to Gumshoe. You and Gumshoe have never met before this and Gumshoe has just become a detective.

- **Crime scene:** Gumshoe was guarding the entrance to the lobby when he heard the gunshot. He saw Detective Badd rush to the scene and they both entered the lobby and discovered the murder. Other than the gunshot, Gumshoe didn't hear anything. **Det. Gumshoe's Testimony** is added to the Organizer.

A bailiff now arrives and says that a Cohdopian Embassy staff member by the name of Manny Coachen has requested to see Calisto Yew. They leave while von Karma arrives. He knows Badd well and is about to let us investigate before we're interrupted by a familiar voice. A younger Franziska is on a vacation from Germany. She sounds as competitive as ever. Von Karma leaves you and Franziska with the investigation, with Detective Badd overlooking them.

Investigation

Franziska challenges you to a competition to find who is worthy of the von Karma name, to which you accept. Detective Badd enters and puts Gumshoe in charge of guiding us. Gumshoe will be your partner from now on.

Detective Badd reveals that the gun used for the murder was taken from Faraday's bag, being one of the pieces of evidence presented at the trial earlier. He says that he knows nothing about the knife, though since Rell was brought in by the police, that must mean the knife belonged to Faraday as well. Badd also theorizes that Faraday attacked Rell first, who then counterattacked.

Examine the **table**. The plastic bags and tea set seems undisturbed, even though a fight just happened. You get the **Neat and tidy table** logic.

Next, examine the **open window**. The bars attached to the **Lobby No. 2 Window** prevent anyone from trying to escape by jumping out. Then examine the **television**. Gumshoe starts messing with it before it suddenly turns on.

Examine the **dead bodies** to enter a close-up scene. Examine the **Plastic bags strewn about** near the body. These are used for storing evidence scattered around the crime scene. Examine the **gun** to get the **Handgun** in your Organizer, then the **bloody knife** to get the **Knife** in your Organizer. Finally, examine **Faraday's left hand**. There seem to be an **Ink stain** on his hand.

We can't find out more with the bodies positioned like this, so after a bit of persuasion from you and a bit of lifting from Gumshoe, we can now examine the scene with their bodies face up. Examine the **object in Faraday's pocket**. Mr. Faraday keeps a fountain pen in his breast pocket. You get the **Fountain pen in pocket** logic. Now examine **Rell's bullet wound**. There are no burn marks around the wound, suggesting that Rell was shot from quite a distance away.
The **Handgun** is updated in your Organizer. Now examine **Faraday's knife wound**. You wonder if the wound matches the knife, so Badd asks a lab tech to verify this. You theorize that Faraday took the gun and the knife from his bag, then aimed the gun at Rell and fired. Rell managed to snatch the knife and stab at Faraday, and both of them died on top of each other. There is

still something not right about these chain of events, though. The **Crime Scene Notes** are jotted down in your Organizer.

Now go into Logic Mode and connect the **Ink stain** with **Fountain pen in pocket**. The ink could have come from the fountain pen, which the lab tech confirms. That must mean that Faraday used his fountain pen to write with his left hand, so he was left-handed. **Mr. Faraday's Fountain Pen** is added to your Organizer. Now connect **Neat and tidy table** with **Plastic bags strewn around**. There is a pile of plastic bags neatly stacked on the table, though a bunch of bags are scattered around on the floor. One bag has some blood on it, which the lab tech verifies as Faraday's blood. The **Plastic Bag** is added to your Organizer.

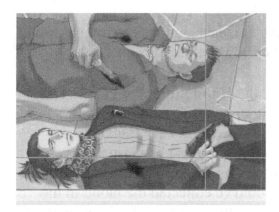

There appears to be nothing left to investigate, though you spot a contradiction in the crime scene. Deduce the **gun** and present **Mr. Faraday's Fountain Pen**. Faraday was left-handed, so why would he hold a gun in his right hand? The only logical conclusion is that someone else was involved in this murder. With that, your investigation is complete!

Detective Badd now gives us the autopsy report. It reveals that Rell lived for a short while after being shot, while Faraday died instantly from the stabbing. The **Crime Scene Notes** are updated in your Organizer. Franziska concludes that she has found the whole truth concerning the case, but we know that there are still some contradictions.

Bad Ending One: If your logic fails here, Manfred comes out and criticizes you of not finishing the investigation in three minutes! Same with Franziska, and he asks both of you to leave. Talk about a speedy investigation in that time limit!

Franziska's Argument: What Happened

1. Mr. Faraday's death was instantaneous, while Mr. Rell survived for a short time.
2. From this, it is obvious that Mr. Faraday died after he shot Mr. Rell.
3. And Mr. Rell, while on the brink of death, stole Mr. Faraday's knife and stabbed him.
4. Those are the facts of this case.

Rebuttal: What Happened

Press the **third statement**. Franziska hesitates while explaining her theory, so you may find a hole in her argument in that part of her theory. You get a new statement.

- They struggled, and Mr. Rell used the last of his strength to counterattack Mr. Faraday.

Present Det. Gumshoe's Testimony at this statement. How could Gumshoe not hear a thing when there was a fight going on behind the door he was guarding? Franziska now assumes that there wasn't a fight and theorizes that Rell stole the knife from Faraday's bag and stabbed him, getting shot by Faraday afterwards. Reply **Yes, something is off** when prompted and present the **Crime Scene Notes**. Faraday couldn't have killed Rell if he was stabbed first!

We're back at our original theory, but there's a contradiction in the crime scene that keeps up from getting the truth, and that is **The order the bodies fell**. If Rell managed to stab and kill Faraday instantly before dying himself, how did he end up below Faraday's body? Although it seems unlikely, Rell must have died before Faraday! Franziska objects, saying that her theory is still correct.

Franziska's Argument: What Happened, Pt. 2

1. It was just chance that Mr. Faraday's body fell on top of Mr. Rell's.
2. The two bodies fell into a pile...
3. ...which indicates that they attacked each other at the same time.
4. It really doesn't matter in the slightest that they fell in the opposite order.

Rebuttal: What Happened, Pt. 2

Press the **third statement** to get a new statement.

- That fact indicates that they attacked each other at the same time from close range.

Present the **Crime Scene Notes** or the **Handgun** at this new statement. The gunshot wound did not leave any burn marks, which means that Rell was shot from at least a few yards away! Franziska wants us to explain who attacked first, so reply **Neither man**. Since claiming Faraday or Rell attacked first will only cause more contradictions, there must be a third person who killed both of them then set the crime scene up. Franziska says we're

missing evidence, but we can totally prove that there was a third person.

Present the **Handgun** or the **Plastic Bag**. Either item points to the presence of a third person. If there wasn't a struggle in this room, there shouldn't be plastic bags strewn around. Using the knife and the bag, the killer could've collected the blood in the bag and scattered some other bags near it to make it look like there was a struggle.

Bad Ending Two: If you lose in this argument, Franziska declares herself the winner as who'll earn von Karma's creed. Some popularity contest!

Yew interrupts you with an "*Objection!*" and requests that Detective Gumshoe is arrested. As the Judge claims that he saw no one in the hallway at a certain point during the recess, Gumshoe could not be guarding the door, and just might be killing the people he was guarding. This could render his testimony, and your train of thought based on it, completely moot. You want to ask one last question before Gumshoe is arrested. Ask him about the **Motive for the murders**. Gumshoe asserts that he has nothing against Faraday, but Yew presents a possible motive.

Yew's Argument: Gumshoe's Motive

1. It was... about a week ago.
2. I saw the detective get chewed out by a livid Faraday in front of the precinct.
3. He stood there super pale, as Mr.

Faraday yelled, "That's a salary cut for you, you nitwit!"

4. A brand new detective suddenly getting his salary cut -- that's reason enough for a grudge.

5. Well? How's that for a "perfect explanation"?

Rebuttal: Gumshoe's Motive

Press the **fifth statement**, and choose to **Raise an objection**. We haven't heard anything about Gumshoe's **Motive for killing Mr. Rell**. Yew says that she has no idea, but claims that if Gumshoe has a reason to kill one of them, he has a reason to kill both.

Yew's Argument: Motive To Kill The Men

1. There's no one out there with a motive to kill both Mr. Faraday and Mr. Rell.

2. All you really have to establish is that someone had a grudge against one of the two men.

3. Mr. Rell, who happened to be there, became a witness to Mr. Faraday's murder.

4. Therefore, he was killed out of necessity, and set up to look like they had killed each other.

Rebuttal: Motive To Kill The Men

Present the **KG-8 Incident Overview** on the **first statement**. There's one man who has a motive to kill both men, and that's Manny Coachen! Detective Badd says that Coachen was in the viewing gallery watching the trial during the murder, leaving Gumshoe as the only suspect. There's nothing you can do to save him.

Talk to Yew:

- **KG-8 Incident:** She claims that she doesn't know anything about the incident other than what was made public, but there is a very clear connection between her and the incident.

Present the **KG-8 Incident Overview** and select that she is connected to it **Through the victim**. The victim's name was Cece Yew, who shared a surname with Calisto Yew. Now she will tell the truth.

- **KG-8 Incident:** Cece Yew was Calisto's sister who was killed by Manny Coachen. Faraday originally had enough evidence to convict Coachen, but a man in black made off with the evidence. Since Manny Coachen was tried before and acquitted, he can no longer be tried again.

- **Manny Coachen:** She confirms that Manny was watching the trial, thus having a solid alibi.

Having obtained all of this information, you are one step closer to finding out the culprit. Gumshoe is hiding something, even though it'll incriminate him as the murderer.

Bad Ending Three: If you fail to counter Yew's argument, Badd asks Gumshoe to come along quietly.

Part 4-2 - Middle

With the suspect and prosecutor of the case both dead, the trial of Deid Mann's murder will be prematurely dismissed. You still wish to continue the investigation, to which Manfred approves. Franziska reminds you that the competition is still on. You won't get anything useful from Gumshoe, so **talk** to Calisto Yew. She says that she was in the Defendant Lobby No. 1 discussing something with Detective Badd when she heard the shot, so you now know that both Badd and Yew have an alibi.

- **Detective Badd:** Detective Badd was also involved in the KG-8 Incident. He was in charge of protecting Cece Yew, but he failed.
- **Time of the murder:** Both Badd and Yew were in the No. 1 Lobby, which makes them unrelated to the crime.
- **Mack Rell:** She only defended Rell because he claimed to be the Yatagarasu. She had no intention of defending him for the murder, but soon found out that he was not the real Yatagarasu.
- **Yatagarasu:** The Yatagarasu steals information about corrupt dealings from companies.

Now that Detective Gumshoe has calmed down, you can **talk** to him:

- **Motive for murder:** He'd mistakenly reported at his old post instead of the Criminal Affairs Department during his first day and thus got scolded for being late by Faraday.

- **During the recess:** Detective Badd ordered him to stand guard in the hallway at around 3:20 pm.

- **Next step:** Gumshoe just received his Annual Bonus Check and cashed it. He had no cash at all before he cashed the five dollars. The **Annual Bonus Envelope** is added to your Organizer.

Present **Det. Gumshoe's Testimony**. Gumshoe asserts that he saw no one in the hallway. Suddenly, the little girl from before sneaks up and kicks you in the legs! She drops a **Swiss Roll** while running away, which is added to your Organizer. You've learned all you can from Gumshoe, so head to the hallway through the left door.

Investigation: Hallway

Both Detective Badd and the Judge are in the hallway. **Talk** to the Judge first:

- **Time of the murder:** He had to go the restroom during the recess. The window at the men's bathroom gives a good view of the hallway by another window at the end of the hallway. He saw Gumshoe buying something from the vending machine, but he disappeared when the Judge looked again.

Now **talk** to Detective Badd:

- **Detective Gumshoe:** He needed someone from the precinct to protect Faraday, since he was just accused of being the Yatagarasu, and got Detective Gumshoe. They met up on the first floor and Badd took Gumshoe to the hallway. Upon entering, he saw Yew, who told him that Faraday had just dragged Rell into the Lobby No. 2, and told them not to disturb the two. Badd ordered Gumshoe to stand guard and heard the gunshot about thirty minutes later in Lobby No. 1 with Yew. Gumshoe never left the hallway, as confirmed by a guard standing at the entrance of the hallway.
- **The gunshot:** He rushed to the scene in less than a minute as soon as he heard the shot.

When prompted about what is interesting here, choose **Time he heard the gunshot**. Detective Badd heard the gunshot right before the trial. **Det. Badd's Testimony** is added to your Organizer.

Examine the **Vending machine**. It sells an assortment of snacks, including Swiss rolls. Examine each snack for some humorous dialogue, but there's nothing else we can find out from this machine right now.

Back up and examine the **window**. Then examine the **Pink piece of trash**. It appears to be made of rubber. Examine the **Windowsill cactus**. It has sharp needles, enough to prick your hands.

Pan down and examine the **ants**. They are gathered around some **Swiss roll crumbs**. Examine the **handprint** on the bench. After some forensic work, you discover it belongs to Detective Gumshoe! **Det. Gumshoe's Fingerprints** are added to the Organizer.

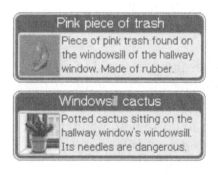

Now go into Logic Mode and connect the **Vending machine** with **Swiss roll crumbs**. There's a strong possibility that the crumbs came from a Swiss roll bought from the vending machine in the hallway. Detective Gumshoe might have been eating a Swiss roll and accidentally dropped some crumbs on the floor. **Det. Gumshoe's Fingerprints** are updated in your Organizer.

If Detective Gumshoe did buy the Swiss rolls, that creates a contradiction. Examine the **vending machine**. Deduce the **Swiss roll price** and present **Annual Bonus Envelope**. Detective Gumshoe didn't have any money before he cashed in his $5 bonus, so how did he buy a $6 Swiss roll? The **Swiss Roll** is updated in your Organizer.

Now that that is settled, go back into Logic Mode and connect **Windowsill cactus** with **Pink piece of trash**. We saw a pink balloon earlier and it might have popped because it touched the cactus. The **Balloon Piece** is added to your Organizer. With that, our investigation is complete!

There's is another thing we need to do, which is double-checking the Judge's testimony. Move to the courtroom. Looks like we're going to do something that most lawyers can only dream of: cross-examining the Judge!

Bad Ending Four: If your logic fails here, Badd forces you and Franziska to leave the investigation.

The Judge's Testimony: What I Saw At Recess

1. During the recess... I, um... I went to the restroom.

2. There is a window on the hallway side. In other words, I could see into the hallway.

3. As I entered, I saw that detective buying something from the vending machines.

4. But when I was about to exit the restroom, he had completely disappeared!

5. A detective that goes missing while on duty... That sounds mighty suspicious to meeeee!

Rebuttal: What I Saw At Recess

Present Det. Gumshoe's Fingerprints on the **fourth statement**. Detective Gumshoe is likely to have sat down at the hallway bench near the window to eat the Swiss roll he just bought. The hallway window is quite high on the wall, so Gumshoe wouldn't be seen if he was sitting on the bench! The Judge now says he recalled something.

The Judge's Testimony: What I Saw, Pt. 2

1. I suppose it's possible you can't see a seated person from the restroom window.

2. However, that doesn't mean that the Detective was sitting there when I looked!

3. Anyway! I forgot to testify earlier

about probably the most important detail...

4. As I was leaving the restroom, I heard the loud "BANG!" of a gunshot.

Rebuttal: What I Saw, Pt. 2

Press the **second statement**. The Judge says he went to the restroom about twenty minutes before the court was to start. A new statement is added:

• Let's see... I looked into the hallway about 20 minutes before we were to reconvene.

Present Det. Badd's Testimony on this statement. Detective Badd heard the gunshot right before the trial started, but the Judge claims he heard it twenty minutes before. **Present** the **Balloon Piece**. The gunshot the Judge heard was actually a balloon popping!

You now recall the small exchange with the little girl. She had a balloon with her and exchanged a dollar bill for a few coins from you. It might just tie everything in this case together...

The Judge attempts to release Gumshoe from arrest, but you say that his innocence is still not completely certain, and now interrogate Gumshoe. It is obvious he's lying, and you'll have to drag the truth out of him.

Gumshoe's Testimony: While I was on

Duty

1. I came down here to this courthouse on Detective Badd's orders.
2. As soon as I got here, he ordered me to stand guard in front of Lobby No. 2.
3. From that time on, until I heard the gunshot, I was in the hallway the whole time!
4. On my honor as a detective, I swear it wasn't me, pal!

Rebuttal: While I was on Duty

Press the **third statement**. Gumshoe insists he was standing guard the whole time, but you know that's not true. A new statement is added:

• And until I heard the gunshot, I didn't take a single step away from the Lobby No. 2 door.

Present the **Swiss Roll** or **Det. Gumshoe's Fingerprints** on this statement. If Gumshoe was standing guard the whole time, he couldn't have bought a Swiss roll or dirtied the bench. Gumshoe confesses that he bought a Swiss roll to eat but there's still something incorrect. Even though it is very clear he couldn't afford it, Gumshoe asserts that he bought the Swiss rolls himself.

Present the **Swiss Roll**. This roll is dropped by the little girl from before. There are two rolls in one package, so he could've given it to the little girl. That same girl tries to sneak up on you again but you dodge. She now introduces herself as none other than Kay Faraday, Byrne Faraday's daughter.

Talk to Kay and present the **Swiss Roll**. She did drop it and was saving it for her dad all along, before breaking down into tears. You offer your cravat to dry Kay's tears but she blows her nose on it! Talk to Kay again.

- **Your father:** She admires her father as a prosecutor and keeps a notebook about the promises she aims to achieve. The **Promise Notebook** is added to your Organizer.
- **Dick Gumshoe:** She did, in fact, meet Gumshoe in the hallway.
- **Swiss Rolls:** She wanted a pack of Swiss rolls but only had a dollar.

You now lend the dirtied cravat to Kay (which will get returned seven years later).

Now to find out why Gumshoe chose to hide the fact that he didn't tell us about the Swiss rolls, though it should be pretty obvious now. **Present** the **Promise Notebook**. One of the promises Kay made with her father is not to take things from a stranger. Gumshoe's just trying to cover for Kay breaking one of her promises!

Gumshoe finally tells the truth. He was hungry while on guard duty, but the cheapest item on the vending machine costs $6, while he only had $5. Kay also wanted to get a pack of Swiss rolls to share with her dad, but only had $1 in coins. So, she and Gumshoe pooled their money together to buy a pack of Swiss rolls. He promised not to tell the others about Kay breaking her promise. They both sat on the bench to enjoy the Swiss rolls but Kay popped her balloon on purpose to surprise Gumshoe, although this caused him to drop his roll. She later tried to give Gumshoe her roll to make up for it but ended up kicking you for questioning Gumshoe.

Yew now enter the courtroom. She says that because you've proven that Gumshoe was in the hallway the whole time, he is the only one who could've committed the murder! If you can't clear his name, Gumshoe will surely get arrested. There is one last place you haven't investigated yet, and that's the Defendant Lobby No. 1.

Part 4-3 - End 1

Now in Defendant Lobby No. 1, you overhear a conversation between Kay and Detective Badd; it seems she found something. Kay leaves the room, and you are free to look around. **Talk** to **Detective Badd**. You mention a strong fragrance that you smelled as soon as you entered the lobby. Badd says that it's the smell of Yew's perfume, which she spilt. **Ms. Yew's Perfume** is added to your Organizer.

- **During the recess:** Until Detective Gumshoe's arrival, Badd and Yew were in separate locations. They were only together after Badd assigned Gumshoe to guard duty. Detective Badd also reveals Yew's and his connection with the KG-8 Incident.

- **KG-8 Incident:** Byrne and Detective Badd were on the trail of a smuggling ring. The sole witness of the smuggling incident, Cece Yew, was killed. Colin Devorae was arrested as the smuggling group's ringleader, but in reality, he knew nothing about the group yet confessed anyway. Manny Coachen was acquitted of the murder of Cece. Badd was supposed to keep Byrne's evidence, which was stolen by an unknown individual. Badd himself has even been involved in a gunfight that left the very bullet holes in his jacket.
- **Relation to Yew:** Badd first met Calisto at the end of the KG-8 Incident's trial. She holds obvious resentment towards him and Byrne, as they couldn't protect her sister. They met her again during a trial involving the smuggling ring. She was the defense attorney for the trial, though she really became one just to find out more about the ring.
- **Relation to Faraday:** Badd met Byrne when he was still a rookie, and was acquaintances with him when Kay was born. They worked on the Yatagarasu case together and gathered a lot of information. Badd was called to testify during this trial about the Yatagarasu.
- **Yatagarasu:** There are three reasons why the Yatagarasu always eludes capture: they always knows the exact location of the target object, they always knows exactly how to disarm the

security system, and they never leave evidence behind. However, in this case, evidence of the smuggling ring was directly sent to the police by the Yatagarasu. Whenever the Yatagarasu wants to publicize a piece of information, it sends it with a special white card.

The bailiff comes and informs us that the Judge is transferring all the evidence we need to us.

Bad Ending Four: If you run out of logic here, Badd believes the investigation has run for too long, and forces you and Franziska to leave.

Bad Ending Five: If you run out of logic with the Judge in the courtroom, the Judge announces that he has to prepare for his next court hearing but will arrange for Gumshoe's arrest. You protest, but the Judge sees no need to further prolong the issue and adjourns the court. Does this sound familiar from Ace Attorney courtroom dramas? The Judge has a quirky personality after all.

Bad Ending Six: If you run out of logic while talking to Gumshoe or Kay, Yew and Badd comes in to arrest Gumshoe due to having enough evidence to warrant it.

New evidence

You arrive in the courtroom and prepare for the evidence transferal. Yew is still busy with her investigation, so there will be no lengthy discussion or analysis. All the evidence is placed on the prosecutor's bench.

Examine the **evidence**. We have the knife, the gun, the documents related to the trial, and Byrne's organizer! Examine the **organizer**. It seems that Byrne was sure that Rell was the killer and that he wasn't the Yatagarasu, as well as having a definitive piece of evidence called the Yatagarasu's Key. **Mr. Faraday's Organizer** is jotted down in your Organizer. There is also a picture of the **Yatagarasu's Key**, which is added to your Organizer.

Now **examine** the **knife**. Byrne never mentioned anything about the knife in his organizer, so what was it doing in his evidence bag? However, there was a mention of something else that no one has seen. **Present** the **Yatagarasu's Key**. The key might just be the knife! You automatically examine the knife. Check the **handle** of the knife. The handle can, in fact, be opened up into a key! The **Yatagarasu's Key** is updated in your Organizer.

Since it appears that even Byrne was not aware of this feature, that means that the killer must have a bigger understanding about the evidence the Yatagarasu sent than Byrne, none other than the Great Thief themselves! That also rules out Rell as Byrne's killer, as he couldn't have known about the hidden blade. The **Knife** is updated in the Organizer.

Now examine the documents and gun to notice that the surveillance video of the murder presented at the trial is still missing. The Judge says that it wasn't found in Byrne's bag, so maybe it's somewhere in the crime scene.

Back at the scene of the crime, we witness Badd talking with another officer. His theme music and attitude should be familiar to you. Badd says that he is Agent Lang from the Republic of Zheng Fa, who is still a rookie cop. **Talk** to **Badd** and **present** either the **Knife** or the **Yatagarasu's Key**. Seems Badd didn't know about the key's trick, either.

- **Time of the murder:** Badd is getting tired of repeating his testimony, but agrees to give it once more.

Badd's Testimony: Det. Badd's Movements

1. ...I was in Lobby No. 1... talking with Yew.
2. ...We were talking about... some trivial things.
3. ...I heard the gunshot... right before the trial was about to reconvene.
4. When we heard it, Yew and I immediately dashed out into the hallway together.
5. I saw Gumshoe goofing around there... and then we all ran into Lobby No. 2.

Rebuttal: Det. Badd's Movements

Press the **third statement**. Badd says that he heard nothing weird before the gunshot. You have him add this to his testimony:

- ...I didn't hear any other strange sounds... until that gunshot...

Present the **Balloon Piece** on this statement. The Judge clearly heard the balloon pop while he was in the hallway, so why didn't Badd hear it when he was in Defendant Lobby No. 1? Badd says that the walls, doors and curtains of the courthouse are soundproof, meaning that he couldn't hear the balloon popping if he were inside the lobby! Using that logic, that means Gumshoe and Badd couldn't have heard the gunshot because the walls were soundproofed.

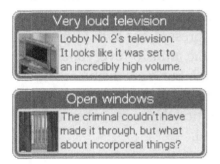

You now recall the states of the crime scene. The window in Defendant's Lobby No. 1 was open for **Dissipating the smell** of Yew's perfume. There is a **Very loud television** in the Defendant's Lobby No. 2. There is a piece of **Missing evidence**, the surveillance video, which wasn't found in the evidence bag.

Armed with these new pieces of logic, you automatically enter Logic Mode. Connect the **Lobby No. 2 window** with **Dissipating the smell**. Since the perfume can be smelled in Lobby No. 2, that means that incorporeal objects can pass through the bars of the **Open windows**! Now connect the **Very loud television** with the **Open windows**. Since smell can past through the window, so can sound! The windows of Lobby Nos. 1, 2 and the hallway were all open, so the sound of the **Gunshot could be heard** by Gumshoe and Badd. Finally, connect the **Missing evidence** with **Gunshot could be heard**. The video captured the exact moment of the murder, including the gunshot, so it can still be left in this very room! Time to examine the television.

Investigation: Defendant Lobby No. 2

You automatically start in a close-up scene of the television. Examine the **video player**. There is a tape inside, and it is confirmed as the missing tape! The **Surveillance Video** is added to your Organizer.

Highlight the **open window** and **deduce** from the **Surveillance Video** that, because the windows in both lobbies and the hallway were open, some witnesses heard the gunshot. The killer purposely opened the window to manipulate the perception of **When the crime took place**. The gunshot that the detectives and Yew heard was from the surveillance video, and the murders must have happened during the recess but before Gumshoe's guard duty. The killer is someone without an alibi during that period.

The bailiff now tells you that Yew has uncovered the real murderer and wishes to clarify something with you. She is waiting in the courtroom. This case is close to being solved, and the confrontation with Yew will likely yield the truth.

Part 4-4 - End 2

ou arrive in the courtroom, and after a brief encounter with Kay, you take the prosecutor's bench. Yew says that her investigation confirmed that there was no way to escape from the hallway, thus she concludes that Gumshoe is the killer. You already know that and a lot more, so you should be able to find the real murderer. The stage is set for a faceoff between prosecutor and defense attorney, but this time, you're on the prosecution's side.

Yew's Argument: Ms. Yew's Argument

1. Everyone, sans the suspect, has an alibi for when the gun went off.
2. Furthermore, the areas around the crime scene have all been thoroughly investigated, right?
3. I also confirmed that there is no possible escape route from Lobby No. 2.
4. Which leaves us with one unshakable conclusion, that Detective Gumshoe is the killer.

Rebuttal: Ms. Yew's Argument

Press every statement. You don't really need to reveal what you know right now, and Yew might have a hidden trump card. Pressing the statements yields nothing new, so it's time you present our own trump card. You ask about the alibis of everyone before Gumshoe arrived, but Yew dismisses it, saying that Gumshoe's the only person who could've committed the crime when the gunshot sounded.

You now present the possibility that the timing of the gunshot was manipulated. Present the **Surveillance Video**. As you learned in the previous chapter, the video was used to fabricate the gunshot and the murders happened much earlier.

Yew now says that the courtroom walls were soundproof, so using the tape's gunshot would not have mattered because nobody could hear it. When prompted, choose **The window was open**. Again, you know that the sound can pass through open windows. The window in Lobby No. 2 was opened by the killer, but the window in Lobby No. 1 also happened to be open. Someone had the window opened because they wanted to have witnesses to hear the fake gunshot. This person is our killer, and said killer is **Calisto Yew**! Yew isn't intimidated by your accusation, and presents a rebuttal.

Yew's Testimony: Ms. Yew's Rebuttal

1. You argue that the window was opened, however, do you have any proof it was I who did that?
2. Furthermore, do you have proof that the tape was used in committing the crime?
3. Frankly, I'm shocked at you for going around accusing people of murder like this.
4. Especially with logic as full of holes as yours!

Rebuttal: Ms. Yew's Rebuttal

Present Ms. Yew's Perfume on the **first statement**. Yew spilled the perfume while she was with Detective Badd in Lobby No. 1. She probably knew that Badd was going to open the window to let out some of the strong smell. In fact, the reason she called Badd into Lobby No. 1 could be to set up an alibi for herself. Yew says she is getting tired of this, and gives you one last testimony.

Yew's Testimony: Why It Couldn't Be

Me

1. Accusing someone of murder over a spilled bottle of perfume is a bit over the top.
2. But I suppose forgery of evidence is to be expected of a disciple of Von Karma.
3. In any case, it simply could not have been me who killed Mr. Faraday.
4. After all, I don't even know where the knife that was used to kill him came from.

Rebuttal: Why It Couldn't Be Me

Press the **fourth statement**. Yew's logic hangs on the fact that she didn't know where the knife came from. She knows the only thing Byrne didn't present in the trial was a key. We already know about the trick with the Yatagarasu's Key, but Yew just revealed something much more important. You get another statement out of her.

- There was a key in his evidence bag, but you can't kill anyone with a simple key!

Present the **Knife** or the **Yatagarasu's Key** at this statement. The key can turn into the knife used in the murder, so as long as Yew knew about the existence of the key, she could've committed the murder. More importantly, not being a member of law enforcement, she shouldn't even have known about the key in the first place. It was sent to the police by the Yatagarasu and only Badd and Byrne could've known anything about it. Yew claims that Byrne told her about the key and the trick within it, but how could he have told her when Byrne himself did not know this trick? Badd also didn't know, so it's not something Byrne would purposely hide from Yew. There was only one person who knew about the key-changing trick, and that's the **Yatagarasu**. Calisto Yew is the Great Thief Yatagarasu!

Yew breaks down into a fit of laughter. She finally confesses to both being the Yatagarasu and committing the double murders. She also reveals that her real name isn't even Calisto Yew. Byrne had discovered her identity as the Yatagarasu and she needed to silence him from telling the world about it. She made Rell accuse Byrne of being the Yatagarasu to land him in jail but didn't expect him to be dragged off during the recess. She feared that her plan and her identity would be revealed, so she killed them both. She predicted that Byrne would bring and use the key to prove that Rell wasn't the Yatagarasu, thus giving her a convenient murder weapon. She entered Lobby No. 2 pretending to be curious about the knife, and while her hand was in the evidence bag she transformed it into a knife and used it to stab Byrne. She had Rell set up the crime scene and tape, then ended his life with a bullet. She finally reveals that she is also a member of the smuggling ring and ordered the assassination of Deid Mann.

Her guilt is now certain, but yet the Yatagarasu remains calm. She reveals the reason the symbol of the Yatagarasu has three legs is that it has more than one way of doing its razor-sharp work. She draws a pistol and almost shoots you but misses thanks to a sudden warning by Kay. However, she escapes with the Yatagarasu's Key, chased by Detective Badd. One final gunshot rings outside the courtroom.

Bad Ending Seven: If you can't beat her arguments, Yew laughs hysterically leaving you losing your cool. Gumshoe gets arrested and Yew declares that she's done with this case.

What really happened

Calisto Yew is actually the Great Thief Yatagarasu, who infiltrates companies to publicize corrupt dealings. Hypocritically, she is also a member of the smuggling ring involved in the KG-8 Incident. Mr. Faraday learned about her true identity while he was investigating both cases, so Yew had to eliminate him.

Yew ordered Mack Rell to assassinate Deid Mann, a witness of the smuggling ring at the Cohdopian Embassy. She also infiltrated the embassy on the same day and sent the Yatagarasu's Key to the police, knowing that it can be turned into a knife. Rell was caught soon after the murder due to being caught on tape but Yew offered to be his defense attorney. She made him claim that he was the Yatagarasu, thus causing Mr. Faraday to bring the Yatagarasu's Key to the court as evidence.

During the trial, Yew made Rell accuse Mr. Faraday of being the Yatagarasu to try and get him arrested. However, she didn't count on Faraday dragging Rell into his office. She feared that her plan would be ruined if Rell was with Mr. Faraday for too long but she still had the key as part of her backup plan. She entered the lobby pretending to be worried about something, silently turned the key into a knife and stabbed Mr. Faraday while the knife was still in the evidence bag, killing him and collecting his blood in the bag.

Yew then ordered Rell to help set up the crime scene by scattering the bags, setting up the tape and opening the window. She killed Rell afterward with the very gun that he used to kill Mr. Mann to remove the sole eyewitness. Yew had a plan to set up an alibi for herself. With the surveillance tape of the footage running and thirty minutes before the gunshot in the tape was fired, she left the room and noticed Detective Badd with Gumshoe. She dragged Badd into Lobby No. 1, making Gumshoe stand guard outside Lobby No. 2.

While standing guard, Gumshoe met Kay Faraday who was looking to buy a snack for her and her father. However, they didn't have enough money to buy the cheapest item on the snack machine, the $6 Swiss rolls. Gumshoe decided to pool his money and Kay's and buy it together. Kay had to exchange the coins she had with a dollar bill, which was how we met her the first time. While enjoying the Swiss rolls, Kay popped her balloon on purpose, which startled Gumshoe and made him drop his Swiss roll. The Judge heard the sound

while in the toilet facing the hallway, mistaking it for a party popper or a gunshot.

As the tape was about to reach the part with the gunshot, Yew purposefully spilled her perfume. As the perfume had a strong smell and spread very quickly, it overwhelmed Badd and made him open the Lobby No. 1 window to let out the perfume. Now both the Lobby No. 1 and 2 windows were open and the tape had reached the part with the gunshot. The sound of the shot was absorbed by the thick walls of the courthouse but it did manage to pass through the windows in both lobbies. Badd heard the gunshot, thinking it was the real deal, and hurried to Lobby No. 2 where he found Faraday and Rell dead. Yew also created a false alibi for herself and a witness that could account for her location during that time.

Epilogue

Badd failed to catch Yew but the precinct has already set up a perimeter around the courthouse. Gumshoe is, of course, found innocent. Badd notes that we might meet again before returning to investigate. Gumshoe thanks us for saving him. You recall that Kay left Gumshoe a present, something that signifies their friendship. **Present** the **Swiss Roll**. It was bought by Gumshoe and Kay, and while the roll she saved never reached her father, she did make up for dropping the one Gumshoe was having. Gumshoe now declares his loyalty to you, which remains evident even to the present day.

Back at Gatewater Land, seven years later, we have encountered Kay once again. She explains that she went to live with her mother's relatives after the death of her father, so she couldn't visit very often. You immediately question why Kay calls herself the Yatagarasu when the real Yatagarasu killed her father. Kay reveals that she found her father's diary while combing through his bookshelves and discovered that he was actually the Yatagarasu. Byrne also had the Little Thief which he used during infiltrations. Despite this, the Yatagarasu has been recently spotted again, as they sent a calling card to the Cohdopian Embassy. Could this mean that Yew has come out of hiding? Kay sought you out to get your help in catching Yew at that embassy.

You're now left with more questions. Who is the real Yatagarasu, Calisto Yew or Byrne Faraday? What caused the Yatagarasu to re-emerge after a seven-year break? Now that you've made your promise with Kay to capture Yew at the embassy, you might finally unravel the truth.

TURNABOUT ABLAZE

Part 5-1 - Beginning

You relax in your office, recalling the events that happened over the last few days. First, you found himself involved in the murder of an Interpol agent on your return flight, then you had to investigate a kidnapping and a murder at Gatewater Land. Finally, in the early hours of this morning, your office became the crime scene of yet another murder, the one of Detective Buddy Faith, along with a thief that made off with a file for an old case.

Just when you are finally going to get a rest, Kay bursts in about the Yatagarasu. You mention that the thief you met earlier could be the Yatagarasu, but Kay believes she will appear at the Cohdopian Embassy today. The Yatagarasu sent a calling card to the embassy, which is odd considering how the card is usually only sent to the media after the Yatagarasu has made off with a secret. The card looks to be the real deal, but you recall that there was another card with inverted colours that you found in the first case. Time to investigate.

The Cohdopian Embassy

At the Theatrum Neutralis, a Steel Samurai play is being shown. You and Kay mention how this embassy is shared by two countries with the theatre as the neutral zone. The Steel Samurai show was sponsored by the Kingdom of Allebahst. Another show, the Jammin' Ninja, is being sponsored by the Republic of Babahl.

(Check out Phoenix Wright: Ace Attorney - Justice For All if you want to know more about these two!) The embassy is holding an event called "The Kingdom of Allebahst versus The Republic of Babahl Goodwill Jubilee". Both countries used to be a single country called the Principality of Cohdopia, but was recently split into two due to civil unrest. Manny Coachen, the suspect of the murder case of the KG-8 Incident, was a staff member of the Cohdopian Embassy seven years ago, and so was Deid Mann.

Both countries had bad relationships with each other, but they're trying to make up for it with this event. Each country also claims to own the real Primidux Statue so they're having them publicly evaluated today. With nothing else to do until the Yatagarasu makes its move, go around and examine your surroundings. You can even find our old acquaintance Lotta Hart making a cameo appearance here! If you talk to the guards, you'll notice how Allebahst has stricter procedures for entry, while the Babahl guards are friendlier and more welcoming. Check the **pile of pamphlets** beside the two women to learn more about the embassy. **Embassy Guide** is jotted down in your Organizer.

Suddenly, the Steel Samurai makes an appearance along with his son, causing a great hubbub. Talk to the **Steel Samurai**. While he doesn't speak to you, he does give you his autograph. **Steel Samurai's Autograph** is jotted down in your Organizer. He then enters the Allabahstian side of the embassy to meet with the ambassador. Now the Jammin' Ninja

segment will begin, who will later enter the Babahl side and meet with its ambassador.

Before we can go any further, though two officers run out of the Allebahstian Embassy and announce that the Yatagarasu has been spotted there! Kay attempts to go there but is stopped by the guard. She then runs over to the Babahlese side to try and climb over the wall and into the Allebahstian side, despite your objection.

At the Babahlese side, Kay is nowhere to be seen, but the fence looks too high to scale across. However, there's a larger problem here. The embassy is on fire and Kay could be trapped inside!

A murder

You enter the Babahlese secretariat's room to find that Kay has been apprehended by Shih-na! Gumshoe is also here, and he directs your attention to a dead body. Kay says that she found the man already dead and she only ran into the room after seeing a suspicious person with a long black coat and a hood over their head enter it too.

Shih-na thinks that Kay committed the murder and there's nothing you can do about it. The crime happened at the Babahlese Embassy, meaning that anything that happens there is subject to jurisdiction by the Babahlese law system, giving them extraterritorial rights. Franziska arrives with the ambassador of Babahl, Colias Palaeno. You request to join Franziska's investigation as her assistant and she eventually agrees. Because Franziska is working with Interpol and you're now her assistant, you can start investigating!

Investigation: Secretariat's Room

You start by asking why Gumshoe is here. It turns out that he was on guard duty for the embassy to watch out for the Yatagarasu. Examine the **dead body**. The victim is Manny Coachen, a familiar name. His death was caused by a stab to the neck from behind. Luckily, the fire did not reach the body. The **Notes on Coachen's Body** are added to your Organizer. You now enter a close-up scene of the corpse.

Examine the **knife**. Tests have shown that the blood on the knife matches the victim's, so it might be the murder weapon. The handle has an exquisite butterfly motif. You get the **Motif on knife handle** logic and have the **Knife** added to your Organizer. Now **examine** the **object** in the victim's pocket. It's the Yatagarasu's Key, stolen seven years ago! Gumshoe doesn't know about its secret, so show it to him. **Examine** the **tip of the handle** to turn it into a knife. The **Yatagarasu's Key** is added to your Organizer. The knife-edge has been cleaned, and you recognize the vine motif on the knife. Franziska suggests talking to Ambassador Palaeno to find out more about Cohdopia.

Talk to **Ambassador Palaeno**. He offers you some coupons, which you recall is part of Babahl's feverish tourist industry.

- **Manny Coachen:** The victim was the secretariat of the embassy, in charge of most tasks in the embassy, one of

which is printing. The embassy has its own printing press because of its need to produce coupons and flyers to promote Babahl's tourism. Ambassador Palaeno also reveals that Mr. Coachen was involved in the KG-8 Incident but soon recovered and worked enthusiastically before he was killed.
- **Renovations:** The embassy was to undergo renovations to give visitors a better impression of Babahl, but the man in charge was the victim.
- **Cohdopia:** Ambassador Palaeno concludes that the key/knife is from the period when both embassies belonged to Cohdopia. It has the motif of the butterfly and the flower, Cohdopia's national symbols. You get the **Key used at Embassy** logic.

Talk to **Franziska**. She is supposed to be working with Interpol around the world, so why is she here? You get the **Franziska's return** logic.

- **The murder:** The Yatagarasu appeared in the Allebahstian Embassy too, but it didn't cause a fire there. Agent Lang is there protecting the ambassador.
- **Yatagarasu:** Franziska doesn't recognize Kay until you remind her about the case seven years ago. Gumshoe brings up the fact that the Yatagarasu is here to steal the embassy's dirtiest secret. You get the **Stealing of secret** logic.

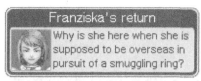

Franziska's return
Why is she here when she is supposed to be overseas in pursuit of a smuggling ring?

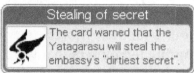

Stealing of secret
The card warned that the Yatagarasu will steal the embassy's "dirtiest secret".

Go into Logic Mode and connect **Franziska's return** with **Stealing of secret**. Franziska thinks that the head of the smuggling ring is right inside this embassy. You gain another dialogue option.

- **Smuggling:** Franziska was indeed on the trail of the smuggling ring and they put the embassy as a prime investigation spot because of a document. It is only part of a set of documents and it's printed with paper only made in Cohdopia, so someone in Allebahst or Babahl must be the head! The **Cohdopian Paper Document** is added to your Organizer.

Now, **examine** the **butterfly symbol** on the wall, which appears to be the **Butterfly of Babahl**, the national symbol of Babahl.

Examine the gold **statue**. This must be the Primidux Statue Kay mentioned; it bears a

resemblance to the Steel Samurai. **Babahl's Primidux Statue** is added to your Organizer.

Examine the **Locked safe** near Kay. You'll need to find the key to open it.

Examine the **knife rack**. The knife rack can be found on the wall on the right side with the burnt shirt and the souvenirs. One of the knives is missing, and Palaeno explains that the handle can be removed.

Motif on knife handle
A butterfly-shaped guard adorns the handle of the murder weapon.

Butterfly of Babahl
National symbol that adorns the national flag. Allebahst's flower is its counterpart.

Locked safe
The secretariat's office safe. It can't be opened without the key.

Key used at Embassy
This key was stolen from the Cohdopian Embassy 7 years ago by the Yatagarasu.

Now go into Logic Mode and connect **Motif on knife handle** with **Butterfly of Babahl**. The knife appears to be part of the Babahlese Embassy, so it may have come from somewhere in this room. Connect **Key used at embassy** with **Locked safe**. The key was used in the embassy before and was found in Coachen's pocket, so it might open his safe. And it turns out it does!

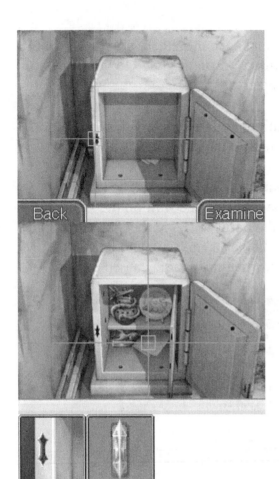

There's nothing in the safe, and it looks like you've just hit a dead end. **Examine** the **piece of paper** at the bottom part of the safe. It seems to be stuck in the safe, somehow... This might mean that **it has two compartments**. The safe does look a bit too shallow compared to its thickness. There don't appear to be any other locks or keyholes, or are there?

Highlight the **hole at the safe's edge** and **deduce** with the **Yatagarasu's Key**. It opened the first compartment, but the key doesn't look like it would fit in the hole. You'll automatically inspect the key; **present** the **tip of the blade**. The knife isn't just a sharp tool, it serves as a

well-disguised key to unlocking the safe's second compartment!

Inside the second compartment are objects that Franziska recognizes as treasures stolen from various countries. More importantly, **examine** the **papers** that were stuck on the edge earlier. They seem a bit familiar. Highlight these **papers** and **deduce** with the **Cohdopian Paper Document** that the smuggling document is, in fact, one of this set of documents. Franziska realizes that Manny Coachen was the head of the smuggling ring, and that he was smuggling large amounts of Babahlese ink.

With that, our investigation is complete!

Shih-na still tries to arrest Kay since you didn't find anything to prove her innocence, but you demand that she explain her reasoning.

Shih-na's Testimony: Why Arrest Kay?

1. Even your police confirmed that the Yatagarasu infiltrated the Babahlese embassy tonight.
2. Utilizing the confusion caused by the fire, the Yatagarasu snuck into this embassy.
3. Furthermore, this girl claims to be the Yatagarasu.
4. And most importantly, there was no one else in here with the body.

Rebuttal: Why Arrest Kay?

Press the **third statement**. Shih-na explains that Kay wanted to steal the documents related to the smuggling case so she killed Coachen to get the key. You get a new statement.

- She wanted to steal documents regarding smuggling, so she killed Mr. Coachen for the key.

Present the **Yatagarasu's Key** or the **Cohdopian Paper Document** on this statement. The key was still on the victim's body when the victim was found and the documents were left untouched. That means the Yatagarasu didn't come here to steal the smuggling documents. Shih-na presents the possibility that Kay accidentally killed Manny Coachen, or that Kay simply did not figure out the key to the second compartment. She even claims that she saw Kay with the murder weapon in her hands when she found the body.

Shih-na's Testimony: Definitive Evidence

1. The knife wound on the body is consistent with the blade of the knife.
2. The knife with the butterfly handle is the murder weapon, which the killer is holding.
3. I assume she obtained the knife from the display rack and used it on the victim.
4. The knife is part of a special 3-piece set, which has a design like no other.

5. The evidence and testimony, it all points to the girl. There is no counterargument.

Kay reveals she followed a suspicious person into the room. It was pitch black when she entered and she felt something on the floor with her hand. After turning on the lights, she let out a scream that alerted Shih-na.

Rebuttal: Definitive Evidence

Present the **Babahlese Knife** on the **second statement**. There's blood all over the blade but none over the handle. The handle is removable, and since there is no blood on it, this suggests that the knife handle has been switched. Examine the **knife's center** to disassemble it. The killer wanted to trick us into believing that they used the Babahlese knife to kill the victim! The **Babahlese Knife Handle** is added to your Organizer. Shih-na counters by saying Kay could've switched the knife, but that's not possible. Examine the **symbol on blade handle**. The symbol is a flower, not a butterfly. Present the **Embassy Guide**. The flower is the symbol of Allebahst, which means that the knife was taken from there! Kay could not have been able to transfer a knife from one side of the embassy to another.

You've successfully cleared Kay's name, but now the biggest question: is how did the knife get here? Before you can ponder the question further, Shih-na interrupts you once more, saying that you still didn't disprove Kay of being the Yatagarasu, and that she could have caused the fire. You'll need to investigate the Allebhastian embassy to get more clues and find out how the knife was smuggled over.

Bad Ending One: If you fail to establish Kay's innocence once your logic runs out, Shih-na stops you from interrupting the investigation and takes Kay into custody. Franziska tells you to expect no mercy from her.

Part 5-2 - Middle 1

You return to the Theatrum Neutralis just in time to witness a humorous scene involving Agent Lang. He isn't too happy that you're here, and he won't even permit you to investigate the Allebahstian embassy. He explains that Allebahst has very strict immigration regulations, so getting permission to enter it is difficult. He also mentions an "incident" that happened at the Allebahstian embassy.

Agent Lang is interrupted by the elderly ambassador of Allebahst, Quercus Alba. He says that he only gave Agent Lang jurisdiction over the investigation in the Allebahstian side to minimise any disruptions, but Ambassador Palaeno arrives to help persuade him. You finally get to investigate the Allebahstian side of the embassy, but Kay and Gumshoe have to stay behind. Before we do that, we should get a bit more information about the smuggling ring.

Talk to **Ambassador Palaeno**. You thank him for his timely assistance, and he even generously gives you some **Babahlese Ink**, made from whitcrystal oil, which is added to your Organizer.

Talk to **Franziska**. She mentions the reason Babahlese ink is not allowed to be brought out of Babahl is because of a batch of counterfeit bills from Zheng Fa made with this ink, making them almost impossible to distinguish from the real ones. The **Babahlese Ink** is updated in your Organizer. She determined that Manny Coachen was the head of the smuggling ring because of the documents of his ink smuggling and the fact that he runs the embassy's printing press. However, neither the bills, the ink, nor the press were found in the Babahlese side of the embassy, so Franziska hopes she will find something in the Allebahstian side. The **Counterfeit Bills** are added to your Organizer.

Now that we're fully prepared, let's enter the embassy! Kay says that she will search for more clues on the Babahlese side, so maybe you'll find something new once you're done with this side.

76

TWO OLD ACQUAINTANCES

Right after entering the Allebahstian ambassador's office, the Steel Samurai suddenly runs into you! After some whipping from Franziska, this mysterious superhero reveals himself to be... Larry Butz, your childhood friend, much to your chagrin. After a brief conversation, Larry reveals that he is once again a murder suspect. Agent Lang soon joins in and says that the victim is a person who sneaked into the embassy, who calls himself Mask☆DeMasque II. Surely enough, the dead body on the floor is wearing a costume that should be familiar to fans of the series.

Of course, Gumshoe worked on the original Mask☆DeMasque case with Phoenix Wright and Maya Fey last year. Play that case to see who claimed to be the real Mask☆DeMasque.

Who's Larry Butz again? There's a saying: when something smells, it's usually the Butz. He is also Phoenix's childhood friend and has a very bad track record with murder cases, which you can see as far back as the series' first-ever case! Larry also appeared in the Mask☆DeMasque case.

As bumbling and useless as he is, Larry isn't someone who would commit murder, so we have to prove that he is innocent. One investigator identified the victim, but Agent Lang won't give us the report.

Detective Badd arrives and asks for the file. He is still chasing after the Yatagarasu after these seven years. You automatically **talk** to him:

- **Initial investigation:** As soon as the Yatagarasu made herself known, Badd and Lang stopped guarding the embassy and started directing things around the crime scene. DeMasque II snuck in during this period of chaos to steal something valuable but was killed when he was discovered by someone.
- **Suspect:** Larry just happened to be the first person they suspected, he's not actually under arrest. Ambassador Alba was to give a speech at the courtyard tonight, but then the Yatagarasu appeared. One person was absent when the Ambassador spoke, and that was Larry. The Steel Samurai cast was to wait in a separate room, but around the time of the murder, Larry was seen on the roof, with one foot in the chimney that leads to this room.

Larry sure has a way of getting into trouble. Without further ado, let's start our investigation!

Investigation: Ambassador's Office

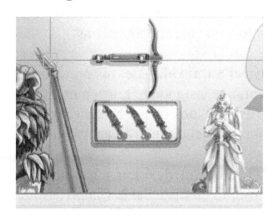

First, **examine** the **knife rack**. An Allebahstian knife was used to kill Manny Coachen, so it must've come from here. **Examine** the **three knives**. One of the knives is missing its blade, which matches up with the blade we have. There's another peculiar contradiction in this scene. Highlight the **spear** and **deduce** with the **Steel Samurai's Autograph**. The spearhead is misshapen, which Larry explains was bent because he was spinning the spear around and hit a wall. He also reveals that the spear is just a prop and isn't strong enough to be used as a weapon. The **Samurai Spear** is added to your Organizer.

Now **examine** the **victim** to enter a close-up scene. **Examine** their **head**. The victim was merely a fake successor of the first DeMasque. His real name is Ka-Shi Nou. He died to being struck on the back of his head. **Examine** the **orange paper** in his hands. There are instructions on how to get to the statue, and it seems that someone requested the victim to steal it. **DeMasque II's Note** is added to your Organizer. **Examine** the **sword**. It belongs to the Steel Samurai, and the blood means it might be the murder weapon. The **Samurai Sword** is added to your Organizer. **Talk** to **Larry** to hopefully get answers to some burning questions.

- **Steel Samurai:** After his previous appearance last month, Larry quit being an artist and took up a job as the Steel Samurai to get close to an actress in the show.
- **Time of murder:** Larry was up on that roof to emulate Santa Claus (despite

it being March, as you point out), but when he tried to climb down the chimney he found that smoke was coming out from it. You get the **Smoke from chimney** logic. It might be the silliest reason to be on the roof ever, but at least it's not murder.

- **Murder weapon:** Larry accidentally left the Steel Samurai sword behind after shaking hands with the ambassador.

Now **examine** the **small table** beside the fireplace. There is a photo of the Steel Samurai shaking hands with Ambassador Alba. The **Photo with Steel Samurai** is added to your Organizer.

Examine the **statue**. It looks the same as Babahl's, but there was only one statue before both countries were split, so one must be the fake. **Allebahst's Primidux Statue** is added to your Organizer. There's something odd about this statue. Highlight the **statue** and **deduce** from the **Photo with Steel Samurai** that the statue had been moved around the time of the crime! **Allebahst's Primidux Statue** is updated in your Organizer.

Examine the **window** to the right of the room. There are two flowers planted here, which Franziska recognizes as passionflowers. The **Passionflowers** are added to your Organizer. Looks like our investigation is complete!

Suddenly, the Pink Princess enters the room. **Talk** to the **Pink Princess**, who reveals herself to be Wendy Oldbag! She was trying to sleep in the other room but came in here after hearing a lot of noise. After running into her two days in a row, looks like you are no luckier than Larry!

- **Pink Princess:** Oldbag was called in by the studio to replace the original Pink Princess actress at the last minute. The **Stand-In Request** is added to your Organizer. However, she also says that she received a **Letter from a Stalker**, which is added to you Organizer. Whoever wrote it got her name wrong, but you seem to recognize the handwriting.
- **Time of the murder:** Around the time of the crime, Oldbag **Used the fireplace** in the next room to warm her hip.

An assistant enters the room to deliver a police dog called Missile. Franziska requested for one to help trace the smell of the Yatagarasu. He goes straight to the fireplace and finds some kind of hot dog, which you say is a Samurai Dog. He eats the whole thing up, so we can't use it as evidence. Missile also found some kind of women's undershirt. The **Lady's Undershirt** is added to your Organizer.

Missile the police dog? Doesn't he look familiar? Well, the other time you see this dog in action is the first game. If you bring the dog to Gourd Lake with a Samurai Dog stand, he eats all the hotdogs, leaving Larry broke! What a laugh!

Given the circumstances, the undershirt can only come from one person. **Talk** to **Oldbag** and **present** the L ady's Undershirt. She confirms that it is hers and that she used the fireplace to dry the sweaty undershirt after the show. She doesn't seem to be lying, so why did the **Undershirt from next door** end up here? Oldbag also confirms that the Samurai Dog was hers.

- **Samurai Dogs:** The Samurai Dogs are a gift from the studio to the embassy, and Larry had to pile them into a cart just to deliver them to the embassy. Oldbag just decided to sample one after the show but managed to finish about half a dozen boxes. The **Samurai Dogs** are added to your Organizer.

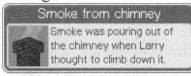

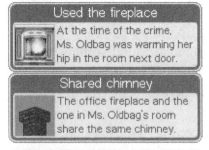

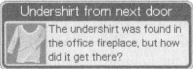

Now go into Logic Mode and connect **Smoke from chimney** with **Used the fireplace**. Because the fireplace in this room was never used, that would mean that the smoke that came out of the chimney in Ms. Oldbag's room next door, which means that these two rooms have a **Shared chimney**.

Then, connect the **Undershirt from next door** with **Shared chimney**. Because Oldbag's room and the Ambassador's office share the same chimney, and Oldbag's undershirt was found in this room, the two fireplaces must be connected.

There's an X in the fireplace here, which makes the wall turn, opening up a passage

to the other room; looks like the two rooms also have a **Connected fireplace**.

With that, your investigation is complete!

Now you need to prove Larry's innocence. Agent Lang is confident that he can counter your arguments, so you'd better come up with a good one. First, you need to find the truth behind Larry's lie, and so you get some testimony from him.

Larry's Testimony: Up on the Rooftop

1. After the show, I left the pushcart in the Rose Garden, and came into the embassy.
2. Then, they took a picture of me shaking hands with the ambassador.
3. After that, and until my next appearance, I had some free time, so I wandered around.
4. That's when I spotted a chimney. A chimney like that is a rare thing, you know.
5. So then, I wanted to play Santa and decided to give it a try.

Larry is still lying, and he claims the reason behind that is because of something embarrassing.

Rebuttal: Up on the Rooftop

Press the **fifth statement** and choose to **Raise an objection**. Santa delivers presents to children, and Larry was certainly intent on delivering something to someone. When asked who that is, **present** the **Ex-Security Lady's profile**. Of course, Larry couldn't have wanted to see Oldbag so badly that he would climb in through a chimney, but what if he didn't know that it was Oldbag? **Present** the **Stand-In Request**. Oldbag was called in at the last minute to replace Mindy, a woman that Larry fancies. Larry tried to sneak into the Pink Princess' room because he thought it was Mindy in the costume. Larry still asserts that that is not the truth.

Larry's Testimony: Larry's Assertion

1. So you think all I wanted to do was to go visit Mindy?
2. Well, I dressed up as Santa and climbed up to the chimney, but the smoke was really thick.
3. It was a case of mistaken identity, and that mistake made me late for the speech.
4. Then, to top it all of, I became a suspect in a murder. THAT'S what you really meant.
5. But why would I ever put myself through so much humiliation on purpose!?

Rebuttal: Larry's Assertion

Present the **Letter from a Stalker** on the **first or fifth statement**. Larry was the one that wrote the letter and was going to "descend upon her from the heavens" if it wasn't for the smoke. Larry had actually intended to meet Mindy, and this letter is proof of it. **Present** the **recipient's name**. Larry had written the name "Mindy" so badly that it looked like "Wéndy"! Larry claims that the letter isn't his, but you can find out if it is through handwriting analysis. While Larry refuses to write anything for you to analyze, he already gave you a piece of his handwriting! **Present** the **Steel Samurai's Autograph**. Larry wrote this for you after the show, so you can use it for the handwriting analysis!

Larry finally confesses and tells the truth to his embarrassing mistake. After seeing the Pink Princess carried by a stretcher, Larry was concerned for who he thought was Mindy. He wanted to visit her but was stopped by the doctors. He then decided to sneak in through the chimney, but not before slipping a letter through the door so that the room's occupant won't be too surprised when he comes down. Although you now know why Larry was on the roof, Agent Lang reminds you that he's still a suspect due to the murder weapon, the Steel Samurai's sword. Looks like you have to deal with Lang, who claims to have got some trump cards from Larry's testimony.

Lang's Argument: Why Larry?

1. I was the one who found the body of the victim, DeMasque II.
2. Beside him was the Samurai Sword... glittering red, and offering up the scent of blood.
3. It was supposed to be in the Steel

Samurai dressing room, but I found it here instead.

4. Plus, I found the murder weapon's owner, the suspect, Larry Butz in here, too.

Rebuttal: Why Larry?

Press the **second statement** to get a revised statement and a new statement.

- Beside him was the Samurai Sword... covered in the victim's blood.
- I suspect he beat the victim to death with that thing.

Present the **Samurai Spear** on the second new statement. The spearhead is bent because Larry accidentally knocked it against a wall. That means that all of the weapons used in the show are hollow, and thus cannot be used to deal a life-ending blow. The sword doesn't even have a dent on it. The **Samurai Spear** is updated in your Organizer. Lang is still not convinced, so you need something that he can't refute.

Lang's Argument: Why Larry? Pt. 2

1. It's possible to use the Samurai Sword to kill someone.
2. And under these circumstances, it's the only logical conclusion.
3. We searched the Embassy, top to bottom, but the victim's blood is only on that weapon.

4. So isn't it only natural that suspicion would fall onto the owner of said weapon?

Rebuttal: Why Larry? Pt. 2

Press the **third statement**, and choose to **Raise an objection**. Lang claimed that his men examined everything in the embassy, but there is one thing they couldn't inspect. **Present Allebahst's Primidux Statue**. Because only the ambassador and the secretariat of the embassy are allowed to touch it, it means that Lang and his men had never laid a finger on it. The photo of the Steel Samurai also shows the statue facing a different direction, which means the statue may very well be the real murder weapon. Lang sends an agent to request permission from the ambassador to let you investigate it, but is denied. Since he isn't here, no one will mind if *you* investigate the statue yourself.

You suggest running a test on the statue using Luminol. The test shows that there is blood on the head of the statue, but that doesn't mean that Larry is innocent. We now examine it in the same way we examine evidence in our Organizer. Check the **bottom** of the statue. There is a handprint underneath the statue, which can be analyzed to reveal the true killer.

After the test concludes, the forensics technician reveals that the fingerprints on the statue belong to the victim of the Babahlese embassy murder, Manny Coachen! If Coachen's fingerprints were found on the statue, that might mean that the two Primidux Statues were switched!

Larry is now innocent, but you're left even more confused than ever. Manny Coachen was killed in Babahl with an Allebahstian knife, while DeMasque II was killed in Allebahst by Babahl's Primidux Statue. There's also the appearance of the Yatagarasu. How do all these facts tie together?

Bad Ending Two: If you fail to prove Larry innocent, Lang ends up arresting him for the murder.

Part 5-3 - Middle 2

You are now outside of the Babahlese embassy, next to the stage. You have left Franziska with the Allebahstian investigation. Now you need to check out the Babahlese Primidux Statue to see if there are any clues about the two statues being moved. You are greeted by the ambassador, Kay, and Gumshoe, though they've not made any progress thus far. You give the **Stand-In Request**, **Letter from a Stalker** and **Lady's Undershirt** to Gumshoe for safekeeping since you don't need those pieces of evidence anymore. You also discard the **Steel Samurai's Autograph**. All of your remaining evidence has been rearranged. If you try to enter the crime scene you'll find that it's blocked, so you can only spend some time looking around this open-air stage.

Talk to **Ambassador Palaeno**:

- **Open-air stage:** The stage is used to host events to promote Babahl. Palaeno planned to give a speech too, after being suggested by Manny Coachen, but the fire prevented that from happening.
- **Primidux Statue:** The statue is said to be a symbol of sovereignty, which is why both countries claim the statue they possess is real.
- **Manny Coachen:** The victim was very good at his job, so good that even Palaeno didn't realize he was involved in a smuggling ring. After Palaeno was selected as the representative of the Country Unification Council, Manny had been working extra hard. Palaeno also reveals that both countries were to remerge tonight if not for the events that had transpired.

Present Allebahst's Primidux Statue. Palaeno has received the news from Franziska and confirmed that the statue in the Babahlese embassy belongs to Allebahst. He also reveals that Allebahst has the real statue and that the rulers of Babahl wanted him to negotiate with Ambassador Alba to fake the results, claiming that the real statue could not be identified.

Now **talk** to **Detective Gumshoe**. He didn't find anything new in his investigation so far.

- **Investigation update:** Gumshoe reveals that Ambassador Palaeno gave him a lantern. The flame is green because the fuel used for the lantern is whitcrystal oil only found in Babahl. There are cutouts on the sides of the lantern that create silhouettes.
The **Silhouette Lantern** is added to your Organizer.

You now recall all the facts of the case and determines that the person that smuggled the murder weapons across both countries must be the fake Yatagarasu, who made her appearance in both embassies. Ambassador Palaeno tells us that the Yatagarasu was first spotted in Allebahst's rose garden where Ambassador Alba was to give a speech. Kay gives us something she found that looks like a guitar **Pick**, which is added to your Organizer. It is slightly wet, but there isn't any water around here. Kay also gives you **Ms. Yew's Perfume** that she found and kept seven years ago, which is also added to your Organizer.

Now that we've just about wrapped up things at Babahl, let's continue our investigation at Allebahst, where the Yatagarasu was first spotted.

Investigation: Rose Garden

You meet up with Franziska back at Allebahst. After exchanging some information, Franziska reveals that the silhouette of the Yatagarasu appeared just as Ambassador Alba was to give a speech. After that, the Babahlese fire started. Without further ado, let's get started!

Talk to **Agent Lang**. He says that he was called back to the Interpol Headquarters for some urgent matter, but he isn't leaving until the murderer is found.

- **Yatagarasu's appearance:** Lang said that he witnessed Yatagarasu's shadow at the same time as the others. The spotlight went on, the shadow was revealed, and the lights went off. When Lang and his men managed to get the lights back on, the Great Thief had vanished. He later found out that the reason the lights went off was that the cord for the electronics was unplugged, either on purpose or by accident. Lang also says that it couldn't have been someone else's shadow, since that shape is unique.

Examine the **pool**. Franziska mentions that the pool's water is used to put out fires. You also observe that the fountain spouts automatically refill the pool until it reaches its normal water level, which means the water must have been used recently.
The **Fountain Spouts** are added to your Organizer.

At this moment, Larry suddenly emerges from the pool! He says that he's trying to find the Iron Infant doll, which he lost around the time he shook hands with the ambassador. He then swims back down into the pool.

Examine the **left statue**. You note its similarity to the Primidux Statue. Examining the **right statue** reveals that it's the statue of a queen. Not much information for you.

After you've done all that, you say that you have figured out how Yatagarasu's shadow was created. **Present** the **left statue**. It doesn't look like the shadow, but that's because the statue is only part of the shadow. **Present** the **right statue**. The Yatagarasu's shadow is in fact, a combination of the shadow of two statues. Some spotlights have been moved during the confusion when the shadow appeared,

which is why it no longer shows the shadow.

You now attempt to recreate the shadow. Combining them looks nothing like the real shadow, so what did you do wrong? The king's statue shadow makes up most of the shadow's shape, but whoever created the shadow only needed part of the queen statue. **Present** her **left hand**. The missing portion from the king statue's shadow has five, thin lines which resemble hands. Rearranging the spotlights so it only shines on the hand makes it look exactly like the shadow we saw. That means the Yatagarasu wasn't in Allebahst tonight, only in Babahl, though we can assume she has an accomplice in Allebahst to set up the shadow. And with that, your investigation is complete!

Bad Ending Three: If you run out of logic here, Lang decides that it's too late at night. He asks you to go home and get some rest as Lang himself is just playing around.

Back where we started

Detective Badd joins you, saying that he left the murder investigation to Agent Lang and wants to focus on catching the Yatagarasu. He said that a woman who claims to be an international journalist (Ace Attorney fans might deduce her to be Lotta Hart) gave him a photo. It was taken from a nearby building after the fires and shows a shadowy figure flying over the wall. The **Photo of Yatagarasu** is added to your Organizer. This is not the first time in the series dealing with flying people... The figure flew from the Babahlese side, so that's where you should head for.

Returning to the theatre, you are joined by Kay. Go right into the Babahlese side. The staff had finished cleaning up the secretariat's office, so maybe you'll be able to get some new clues we previously missed. First, you need to compare the state of the room before and after the fire. Then you need to find out who the mysterious person Kay saw is. Kay seems to recognize the shadow in the photo we just received as that suspicious person. Let's get down to investigating!

Investigation: Secretariat's Office

Talk to **Ambassador Palaeno**. He reveals that two fires broke out tonight. The first broke out during the Jammin' Ninja show and only affected the fourth and fifth floors of the embassy, but was kept secret to avoid causing panic. Detective Badd also mentioned the first fire when he gave us the photo, which means it was taken right after the first fire. The **Photo of Yatagarasu** is updated in your Organizer. The second fire occurred on the third floor, alleged to be caused by the embers on the upper floors

after the first fire. The **Fires in Babahl** are added to your Organizer.

- **Morning activities:** Palaeno was to shake hands with the Jammin' Ninja, but Coachen wanted to turn it into a photo op, so they spent the morning tidying up Coachen's office. The event couldn't be held in the ambassador's office because it was undergoing **Renovations**. This is also why the knife set and the Primidux Statue are in the secretariat's office. Palaeno says that he used the fireplace during the cleanup, accidentally spilling some Babahlese ink on the back wall, and forgot to clean the ashes in the fireplace. **Amb. Palaeno's Testimony** is added to your Organizer.
- **Afternoon activities:** Coachen and Palaeno were together that afternoon, until the start of the Steel Samurai show. Palaeno had to return to his office to get ready for the photo op at the end of the show. After that, he went back to his office, but then the fire broke out and he had to escape down the stairs. This means that Palaeno did not see the victim at all after the Steel Samurai show.

First, **examine** the **table** to enter a close-up scene. **Examine** the **ink bottle**. It is still quite full, and the fire couldn't burn away any of it. Palaeno notes that something is odd about the ink. **Talk** to him about it.

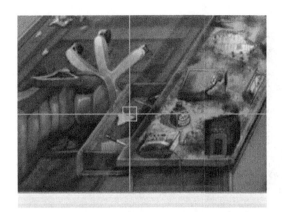

- **Mr. Coachen's ink:** Coachen was worried about his office when the second fire broke out, so he rushed in. Ambassador Palaeno tried to follow him but was stopped by an inferno of green flames when he tried to enter the office. The flames could only have been caused by the whitcrystal oil in the ink, so he was quite surprised when there was still a bottle of ink on Coachen's desk.

Back at the close-up scene, **examine** the **open drawer** to open it a bit more. Now that you can see what's in the drawer, highlight the **orange paper** and **deduce** from **DeMasque II's Note** that the shape and color of the note look exactly like the one we have. Palaeno says that its a souvenir from somewhere in the country. He also confirms that the handwriting on the note is Coachen's. That means Coachen ordered DeMasque II to steal Allebahst's Primidux Statue! **Talk** to the ambassador again.

- **Job for DeMasque II:** Babahl's Primidux Statue was a fake, as we were previously told. Palaeno was concerned about this fact when the statues were to be examined at the end of the event. After consulting the victim, he probably

wrote the note. Why did Coachen want to ensure Palaeno became the ambassador of the reunited Cohdopia, as he himself was more capable?

Detective Gumshoe enters the room, saying that he has all the information about the office before the fire. With this information, Kay can use Little Thief to recreate the state of the room before and during the fire!

Bad Ending Four: If you run out of logic here, Shih-na ends the investigation and asks you and Kay to vacate the premise.

Recreation: Secretariat's Office

First, **examine** the **grandfather clock**. It seems like it was flush against the wall before the fire, but was moved afterwards. Detective Gumshoe finds a length of **Wire** inside the clock that prevented it from chiming, which is added to your Organizer. Someone, likely Coachen's killer, tampered with the clock.

Now **examine** the **knife rack**. It appears that one of the knives had already gone missing before the fire.

Examine the **flames**. Since the flames were out by the time Kay entered the room and because Palaeno could not do the same when the fire was burning, you can assume that the only people that entered after the fire started was Kay and the mysterious person. There is one thing that could be the source of the fire, even though it's not as large. **Present** the **Silhouette Lantern**. The lantern burns with whitcrystal oil, which is probably what caused the fire; Palaeno was

mistaken about the
source. **Present** the **Babahlese Ink**. The
ink also consists of whitcrystal oil, which
was why Palaeno mistook it as the fuel for
the fire. You know that the victim
smuggled a lot of ink, which could be used
to create something flammable, something
that could cause such a large
fire. **Present** the **Counterfeit Bills**.
Coachen was counterfeiting the bills used
in Zheng Fa, and whoever started the fire
used the bills as fuel. The **Counterfeit
Bills** are updated in your Organizer.

Now **talk** to **Gumshoe**. He says that the
first fire took him by surprise and he tried
to escape using the elevator, but it was
being used by someone, so he had to use
the stairs. Palaeno mentions that all staff
members are warned to use the stairs, so
who used the elevator?

- **During the fire:** A mysterious
  person wearing a long coat was spotted
  in the embassy, causing quite some
  panic. It seems to match the figure that
  Kay saw.
- **What you saw:** Gumshoe couldn't
  chase the Yatagarasu because he was
  lost, but soon encountered Kay being
  arrested by Shih-na. Gumshoe also
  mentions that he saw Shih-na coming
  out of the next room when he was
  nearing Kay's location. You get
  the **Shih-na's location** logic.

We have examined everything in this office,
but there is still something that bothers you.
The office looks very similar to
Ambassador Alba's. Palaeno reveals that
both embassies have **Bilateral symmetry**.

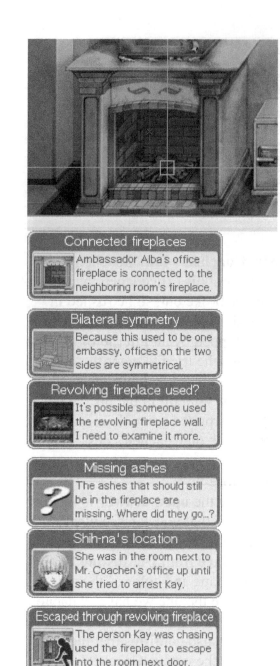

Connected fireplaces
Ambassador Alba's office
fireplace is connected to the
neighboring room's fireplace.

Bilateral symmetry
Because this used to be one
embassy, offices on the two
sides are symmetrical.

Revolving fireplace used?
It's possible someone used
the revolving fireplace wall.
I need to examine it more.

Missing ashes
The ashes that should still
be in the fireplace are
missing. Where did they go...?

Shih-na's location
She was in the room next to
Mr. Coachen's office up until
she tried to arrest Kay.

Escaped through revolving fireplace
The person Kay was chasing
used the fireplace to escape
into the room next door.

Now go into Logic Mode and
connect **Bilateral
symmetry** and **Connected fireplaces**. If
the building is symmetrical, that means this
room's fireplace might also have a hidden
passage. The killer likely used this passage
to escape. You get the **Revolving fireplace
used?** logic.

We are now in a close-up scene of the fireplace. Sure enough, there is an X that activates the revolving wall, but something is missing from this scene. Deduce the **logs** and present **Amb. Palaeno's Testimony**. Palaeno said that he forgot to clean up the ash after burning some files this morning, so where did they go? You get the **Missing ashes** logic. Kay inputs some new information into the recreation, so now the fireplace has the missing ashes.

Go back into Logic Mode and connect **Revolving fireplace used?** with **Missing ashes**. Palaeno also mentioned that he spilt some ink on the back wall, but we can't see any trace of it. This indicates that the revolving wall was used and that both sides had been switched. The **Revolving Fireplace Wall** is added to your Organizer. That means whoever killed Coachen escaped through the fireplace. You get the **Escaped through revolving fireplace** logic.

Finally, connect **Shih-na's location** with **Escaped through revolving fireplace**. Since Gumshoe witnessed Shih-na coming out of the next room, it could mean that she used the secret passage, and that might make her Manny Coachen's killer!

With that, our investigation is complete!

The truth about Manny's murder

You now recall the time Kay was arrested. Shih-na came out of the next room as soon as she heard Kay scream and instantly accused Kay of the crime. However, we need to do something else before confronting Shih-na. You ask Gumshoe to run a handwriting analysis on DeMasque II's note. You also make Gumshoe try and fit through the passage, through the ashes.

You might've figured out who Manny's killer might be, but there are still a lot of unanswered questions. Gumshoe returns from the next room. His jacket is dirty from the ashes and ink, but you now know that someone can move through the passage. You still need the results from the handwriting analysis, though that would take a bit of time. For now, you should wait at the Theatrum Neutralis with Agents Lang and Shih-na.

Part 5-4 - Middle 3

Having deduced the killer of Manny Coachen in the last chapter, it is now time for you to confront Shih-na. You meet Agent Lang, Franziska and Ambassador Alba in the Theatrum Neutralis. It appears that they have yet to find out that the fuel for the fire was the counterfeit bills. Lang is noticeably frustrated because he couldn't catch the leader of the smuggling ring before he died. You still need to question Shih-na. Detective Gumshoe enters the theatre with the results of the handwriting analysis and confirms that the handwriting on DeMasque II's note is indeed Coachen's. **DeMasque II's Note** is updated in your Organizer.

You now demand that Shih-na explain how she didn't see the Yatagarasu when she was only in the next room. Lang steps in to prove Shih-na's innocence, so if you are to find the truth, you'll have to confront him. First, you need to establish that the Yatagarasu visited the Babahlese embassy and find out who was the mysterious person Kay saw.

Kay now gives you her testimony about the suspicious person. She saw the person around the open-air stage, but they ran into the embassy after she called out to them. She chased the person onto the third floor but lost track of them when they went around a corner. She tried her best to catch up, just in time to see the person enter the secretariat's office. When she entered the room and turned on the lights, the person had disappeared.

You ask Agent Lang how the person escaped. While Lang says that they slipped past Kay in the darkness, that couldn't be possible, as if the person did escape that way, the Yatagarasu would have bumped into someone. **Present Shih-na's profile**. Because Kay alerted Shih-na in the next room when she screamed, anyone who tried to escape through the door would have run straight into her. Even if the person managed to elude Shih-na, they would still have bumped into Detective Gumshoe, who was running towards Kay's position from Shih-na's opposite.

Agent Lang still doesn't know about the revolving fireplace in Babahl, so you should keep that a secret for now. He states the window as another possible escape

route and says that the photo seems to prove it. Whoever in this photo could not have been the person that Kay saw. **Present** the **Photo of Yatagarasu**. This photo was taken after the first fire, whereas Kay saw the person during the second fire. Lang demands an explanation for the person's escape route, but you ask Shih-na, the investigator in the Babahlese side, to explain for him in his stead. Shih-na takes the challenge, so you'll start with her movements in the embassy.

Shih-na's Testimony: Shih-na's Movements

1. During the first Babahlese fire, I assisted in putting out the fire.
2. During the second fire, I was searching for the Yatagarasu that had appeared in Babahl.
3. While I was searching, I heard a scream coming from the next room over.
4. Although I was in the next room, I was unable to catch a glimpse of the Yatagarasu.
5. To be honest, I'm actually very skeptical that the girl's "Yatagarasu" even exists.

She doesn't quite believe in Kay's testimony, so you must prove its existence.

Rebuttal: Shih-na's Movements

Present the **Revolving Fireplace Wall** on the **fourth statement**. As you've ruled out all the other possible escape routes, that leaves the fireplace as the only possible path for the suspicious person to take. If Shih-na was in the other room, she should've seen the person. The only explanation for that is that Shih-na was the person Kay saw, and she led her into Coachen's room, escaped through the fireplace and arrested Kay.

The laugh

You've cornered Shih-na, and she seems to be out of words. She suddenly laughs in a very familiar fashion, reminding you of someone seven years ago. Shih-na says that your accusation is merely speculation, with no proof to back it up. You do have proof that the fireplace passage was used recently, though. **Present** the **Revolving Fireplace Wall** or **Amb. Palaeno's Testimony**. Ambassador Palaeno burned some files with Coachen that morning but forgot to clean up the ashes. The ashes weren't in the room when you investigated it because whoever used the fireplace passage pushed the ashes to the opposite room. Shih-na is still not convinced and says that the next testimony will be her last.

Shih-na's Testimony: Shih-na's Rebuttal

1. In my eyes, all you've proved is that the revolving fireplace wall was used...

2. ...but you can't really call that proof that the Yatagarasu used the fireplace, now can you?

3. So then, who was it that used the rotating wall? Show me your answer with real evidence.

4. Remember, we've already finished our very thorough investigation...

5. ...and we found not a single suspicious thing in Mr. Coachen's office.

Rebuttal: Shih-na's Rebuttal

Present the **Counterfeit Bills** or the **Wire** on the **fifth statement**. You found the wire in the grandfather clock at the crime scene. Not only that, but you also found out that someone had burned counterfeit bills in that office! That means that her "thorough" investigation was not very thorough at all. There is also one place that Interpol failed to inspect. **Present Shih-na's room**. She was the only one investigating there, so it is possible that she hid something from you. Gumshoe goes to inspect the next room immediately.

Remember that you had Gumshoe pass through the fireplace passage into the other room and how his coat got covered in ash and ink. Gumshoe returns from his investigation with three pieces of evidence: some make-up, a coat, and a pair of shoes. Shih-na claims that those belong to her, so they can't be considered evidence. However, they are quite significant to the investigation, and Agent Lang permits us to examine her belongings. Choose the **Coat**. It is stained with ash and ink, but Shih-na claims that it was the soot from the first fire she helped put out. She is probably lying, and you know what the dark substance on the hem of the coat really is. **Present** the **Babahlese Ink**. Ambassador Palaeno said that he spilled some Babahlese ink on the back wall of the fireplace and Gumshoe got some of it on to his coat when he tried to pass through the passage. If we can prove that the substance on her coat is ink, that will prove that she used the fireplace! Choose to **Burn the coat**.

You take a piece of the coat and light it on fire, which burns with a green flame. Babahlese ink is made up of whitcrystal oil, which produces a green flame when burned. You now accuse Shih-na as being Calisto Yew, the fake Yatagarasu! **Present Ms. Yew's Perfume**. Kay had preserved the bottle Yew spilled almost perfectly for the last seven years, which means that Yew's fingerprints should still be on it. By conducting a fingerprint test, we can prove if Shih-na really is Calisto Yew.

Shih-na lets out an even longer laugh and finally confesses to being the Yatagarasu. She was sent by the smuggling ring to be a spy, intentionally thwarting all of Interpol's efforts to find their leader. She suddenly holds Kay hostage, saying that she is the true Yatagarasu and asking you why the Yatagarasu has three legs. You now recall a conversation with Detective Badd. The Yatagarasu is always one step ahead because it always knows the exact location of an object, always knows how to disarm the security system, and never leaves evidence behind.

You suddenly realize the real identity of the Yatagarasu. Choose **Neither person**. The Yatagarasu is not one person, but it is actually a team that consisted of Calisto Yew and Byrne Faraday. The Yatagarasu knows the exact location of its target because Yew was able to find out corporate dealings by being a lawyer. The Yatagarasu always knows how to disarm a security system because Byrne knew the ways of a criminal, being an experienced prosecutor.

That leaves us with the final skill of the Yatagarasu: it never leaves any evidence behind. Detective Badd has overheard the commotion and has his gun pointed at Shih-na. He reveals that the reason the evidence was never found is that he, being the lead detective in all the cases involving it, hid them away. Yew has had enough of this whole ordeal and pulls the trigger.

Suddenly, Agent Lang shoves Kay away from Yew and blocks a bullet from

Detective Badd. Even if she is a murderer or a spy, she is still his subordinate, which he has a duty to protect. He requests Franziska to conduct a full-body search to check for other weapons with help from Gumshoe. He finds a blade without a handle, a vital piece of evidence that happens to fit perfectly with another piece of evidence. **Present** the **Babahlese Knife Handle**. It was taken out from the handle when the blades were switched, so you ask Gumshoe to return the handle and blade to Ambassador Palaeno. The blade is concrete proof that Yew is the killer of Manny Coachen.

Shih-na (or Calisto Yew) killed Coachen with an Allebahstian knife, swapped the handle of the blade with one from Babahl and took its original blade with her. Then she lured Kay into the office to try and pin the crime on her. Yew reveals that she wanted to capture Kay to take the Little Thief. Byrne infiltrated this embassy seven years ago using the same device and stole the key. Yew also reveals that the only reason she killed Byrne was that the smuggling ring she belonged in was worried about the Yatagarasu. She hints that the real ringleader is still alive and yet to be arrested, and also reveals that she was the one who started the fires.

Just before Shih-na is taken away, Kay stops her. She says that she found some hair sticks that Shih-na dropped when she was shoved by Agent Lang, but Shih-na lets her keep them. Shih-na also claims that she wasn't Manny Coachen's killer. Lang says that he will return even with a

wounded leg, saying that the case is now a personal one to him.

Bad Ending Five: If you run out of logic here, Lang believes it's a waste of time and takes you off the case.

Epilogue?

Kay lets you keep the **Hair Sticks** for her, which you observe have a bit of soil at the ends, and add them to the Organizer.

Detective Badd is relieved that the whole legend of the Yatagarasu is over, saying that he can finally retire. He returns some files on the KG-8 incident back to you, meaning that he was the thief we encountered in the first case!

Badd reveals that the Yatagarasu started after the KG-8 Incident. After evidence was stolen and Manny Coachen was found Not Guilty, they decided that the law has a limit. They vowed to reveal the truth behind any companies dealing with the smuggling ring. Just as they were about to find out the identity of the smuggling ring's ringleader, Calisto Yew betrayed them and killed Mr. Faraday. After his death, Badd looked into Yew's past and found out that Cece Yew never had a sister. "Calisto Yew" was merely another fake name.

Badd says that he stuck a trump card under a photo in the case files. This card is

93

actually a directives card that Coachen possessed at the time of the KG-8 Incident and had Cece Yew's blood on it. The reason they called themselves Yatagarasu was because of the three-legged raven used by the ringleader of the smuggling group. The cards were orders sent by the boss of the ring and members that received it were required to burn it, producing a green flame. Byrne miraculously obtained the card, so the team decided to use a card with inverted colors as a warning for the smuggling ring. The **Trump Card** is added to your Organizer.

He also gives us the stolen evidence from the case, which was stolen and hid away by Ernest Amano and only found after his arrest. The **Video Tape** is added to your Organizer. Amano had prepared to overthrow the ringleader and had the videotape as insurance. He also instructed Jacques Portsman to steal the video and to infiltrate your office to take the trump card. These two pieces of evidence are, therefore, illegal, but Badd says they will be useful against those that are "above the law". He now asks Gumshoe to arrest him, the last remaining member of the Yatagarasu.

The legend of the Yatagarasu has finally ended, but the case is still not over. Who killed both men, and who is the ringleader of the group?

Part 5-5 - End 1

Even though you've solved the mystery of the Yatagarasu, you still have to find out the truth behind the two murders, such as how the murder weapons crossed borders. Both Allebahst and Babahl have strict regulations on immigration, so it can't be easy smuggling them across. You now re-arrange your evidence and remove some that are no longer useful.

Gumshoe plays the tape Detective Badd gave us on a nearby TV set. It shows Manny Coachen entering a building with a knife and a card in his hands. Franziska deduces that it is the apartment building of the victim of the KG-8 Incident. Someone stole this tape during the trial for the incident. It is important enough that the ringleader of the smuggling group actually wanted it hidden, so there must be something in this video that ties it to the ringleader.

You tell Gumshoe to pause at one scene. It shows a car, and this car does have some relevance to the current case. **Present** the **flag** near the front lights. The flag belongs to the Principality of

Cohdopia, which means a Cohdopian government car stopped there, but why?

Bad Ending Six: If you run out of logic here, Lang proclaims that no-one can take the case away, forcing you and Franziska out of the building.

Ambassador Alba now enters the Theatrum Neutralis. He requests us to stop our investigation temporarily, as the jubilee is still being held. Agent Lang now returns to the embassy searching for us. He says he knows the culprit behind the Allebahstian murder and accuses Franziska on the spot! He says that Alba called Franziska to his office before the speech and that Franziska moved freely between both embassies during the investigation. He requests Alba to let us inspect his office to prove Franziska's guilt.

We must now prove that Franziska didn't commit the murder, or else we won't be able to continue with our investigation at all!

Lang's Testimony: Border-Crossing Weapons

1. One of Allebahst's knives was used in Babahl to murder Mr. Coachen.
2. And the murder weapon in the killing of DeMasque II is Babahl's Primidux Statue.
3. Somehow, these two objects were able to penetrate the two countries' impenetrable security.

4. The only one who traversed the two countries just before and after the crimes was you.

Rebuttal: Border-Crossing Weapons

Present Babahl's Primidux Statue or **Allebahst's Primidux Statue** on the **third statement**. Not only was the knife and Babahl's statue smuggled over, but the one in Allebahst was also smuggled to Babahl.

Agent Lang insists that only Franziska could've done it, but there is someone else who crossed the borders tonight. **Present** the **Photo of Yatagarasu**. Whatever was the thing in the photo went to the other side above the wall between the embassies. Agent Lang says that it isn't humanly possible for someone to fly over it, but why must it be a human? **Present Allebahst's Primidux Statue**. Shih-na could've dressed the statue in clothes and launched it over the border, but how?

You now ask Franziska to testify about her movements when she was called into Ambassador Alba's room.

Franziska's Testimony: Movements in Allebahst

1. As I said earlier, I was assigned to guard duty in the Allebahstian Embassy.
2. After I saw the Steel Samurai off on his way towards the ambassador's office.

3. I returned to the rose garden for a bit, and checked up on the security situation.
4. After all the preparations were in place, I was called back by Ambassador Alba to his office.

Rebuttal: Movements in Allebahst

Press the **fourth statement** to get a new piece of testimony.

- When I arrived, Ambassador Alba was watering the flowers on the windowsill.

Press this new statement to get another piece of testimony.

- There were four large passionflowers in full bloom in the flower box.

Present the **Passionflowers** on this statement. Franziska recalls seeing four passionflowers, but there were only two when you investigated the office earlier. You now investigate the flower box in closer detail.

Examine the **passionflowers**. There are clearly only two passionflowers in this flowerbox, so is Franziska lying? Choose to **Show evidence** when prompted, then **present** the **Hair Sticks**. Shih-na was holding these sticks when she was in Babahl, but they look exactly like the plant supports for this flowerbox! It was also smuggled over the border, but for what reason? **Present** the **crossbow**. These support sticks can also be used as crossbow bolts! Agent Lang says that these sticks could never carry a statue across the border.

Lang's Argument: Border Crossing, Pt. 2

1. So Babahl's statue was draped in the Yatagarasu's clothes, and then shot over here?
2. Even if you fired the arrows from this side, they wouldn't go far with a statue tied to them!
3. I don't think I need to tell you that the Primidux Statue didn't sprout wings.
4. You're a realist, after all, aren't you?

Rebuttal: Border Crossing, Pt. 2

Press the **second statement** to get a new piece of testimony.

- If it wasn't a statue that was tied to the arrows, then what did the crossbow launch...?

Present the **Wire** on this statement. The wire was tied to the sticks then launched to Babahl's secretariat office, so Allebahst's Primidux statue can be ziplined to the other side. That still doesn't explain how Babahl's statue managed to reach Allebahst, having to move two floors higher on its own. There is a certain form of motion that makes this possible, however.
Select **Rotary motion**. Two ends of the wire were sent to Babahl to form a pulley system, so both statues could be transported simultaneously.

Someone shot a wire from Allebahst to Babahl, creating a pulley system to switch both statues, with Shih-na staying in Babahl to help smuggle the statues. Another arrow was fired carrying the other end of the wire into Babahl, where Shih-na hid it in the grandfather's clock.

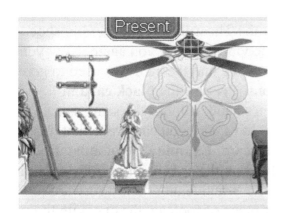

Agent Lang says that this is still not enough to prove Franziska innocent, but you say that there is a piece of evidence in this very room that can be used to provide the rotary motion used for the pulleys. **Present** the **ceiling fan**. There are fans in both rooms with Primidux Statues, which can be used as pulleys.

Bad Ending Seven: If you run out of logic here, Lang arrests Franziska, as he's tired of waiting for everyone to solve this case.

Whoever planned this trick must be someone familiar with the offices of both embassies and know that the support sticks could be used as arrows. It should be obvious who the mastermind is, but a simple accusation will become a major international
incident. **Present** the **Crossbow Arrows** or **Passionflowers**. The arrows used for the crossbows were hidden as passionflower supports, and someone spent the time to grow those passionflowers until even Franziska couldn't recognize it. Whoever did it is also very familiar with the layout of both embassies to know about the ceiling fans. The culprit is Ambassador Quercus Alba!

There is one peculiar thing about the plan if the ambassador hatched it. **Present Allebahst's Primidux Statue**. If the statue in Allebahst is the real deal, why swap it for a fake? You now automatically examine the Primidux Statue.

Examine the **head** of the statue. You note that there is a gap at the neck, which opens it and reveals a bronze object. Examine the **object**. It is actually the plates used for the printing of the counterfeit bills!
The **Counterfeit Plate** is added to your Organizer.

Since only the ambassador or the secretariat of an embassy is allowed to even touch the statues, a fake hollow one could be used to conceal something. After receiving the statue, Alba ran into DeMasque II, who is coincidentally out to steal the statue. Alba tried to intimidate the thief and accidentally killed him with the statue.

Bad Ending Eight: If you run out of logic here, Alba forces everyone to vacate the premises.

Alba admits to smuggling the statue and killing DeMasque II by accident, but asserts that he is not the ringleader. Agent Lang reveals that he was always suspicious of him but he needed his permission to investigate the room. He accused Franziska just so he could investigate the office one more time. Alba now says that you don't have any proof that he is the ringleader, nor do you have any evidence suggesting that he knew about the counterfeit plates.

You're now faced with a difficult choice. You can use the proof that Detective Badd gave us, but that would mean presenting illegal evidence. You'll be given a choice, but you will be forced to present them either way. These two illegal pieces of evidence are what will prove Ambassador Alba as the ringleader of the smuggling ring!

Back at the Theatrum Neutralis, Gumshoe plays the videotape for you again. Now you need to prove that the card was used to give directions. **Present** the **black card** in Coachen's hand. It looks the same as the one you have, and you can prove that it is the same card. **Examine** the **bloodstain**. The blood on the card belongs to the victim of the KG-8 Incident. You fast forward to another piece of footage, the one with the car. The image is magnified, so you can see the person in the car. His face isn't visible, but there is one thing that connects this case with Cohdopia. **Present** the **card** in the person's breast pocket. The shape of the pocket and the card in it confirms that Coachen arrived on that car that day.

Ambassador Alba now reveals his true self, turning from a weak, elderly person to a fearsome ex-army man. He says that Cohdopia no longer exists, so we don't have any records to confirm that Coachen was in that car that day. You can still prove that Alba was in it, though. Present the **reflection of the medal** on the opposite window. The medal reflected off the window in the picture matches the one Alba is wearing right now!

Alba now confesses to killing DeMasque II in self-defense. He says that the man attacked him, so he struck back. He shows you the wound in his shoulder as proof. Alba hid DeMasque II's weapon after the murder, a pair of shears. **Amb. Alba's Wound** is added to your Organizer.

He still says that the smuggling and counterfeiting were all done by his secretary without his knowledge. He also says that he can only be tried at Allebahst due to his extraterritorial rights. Even if he is driven out of this embassy, he can

continue ruling another in a different country, continuing his smuggling activities freely! How do you lay down the law on a man that's untouchable?

This battle of wits has only just begun.

Part 5-6 - End 2

Looks like it's the end of the road for you. Ambassador Alba's extraterritorial rights basically grant him diplomatic immunity, so even if you have the evidence to prove he is guilty, he can't be arrested. Agent Lang leaves us for a moment to take care of some business. You've come this far, so you can't stop here! Gumshoe will investigate Babahl while Franziska will go investigate Allebahst, so you're left with the Theatrum Neutralis. Before you start your investigation, you erase the now useless **Passionflowers** data from the Organizer.

Investigation: Theathrum Neutralis

You recall how Alba seemed to be agitated over something. You get the **Agitated Alba** logic. **Coachen's counterfeiting op.** apparently counterfeited bills using the embassy's printing press because of the extraterritorial rights. Alba himself has a special kind of extraterritorial rights that protects him if he commits any crime in this country, so unless you can somehow remove his status, you can't touch him.

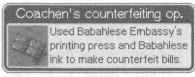

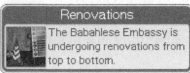

Go into Logic Mode and connect **Renovations** with **Coachen's counterfeiting op.**. The ink and the plates for the counterfeiting must've been stored in a secret location, but once the embassy renovations started, Coachen had to find a new hiding spot or dispose of his tools. So who was most able to benefit from this? **Quercus Alba**, of course. If Manny Coachen was dead, Alba would have all evidence of the counterfeiting erased, ensuring that he would never be caught for this crime; in other words, he had a strong **Motive to kill Coachen**.

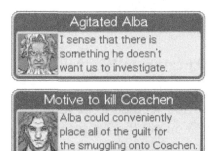

Next, connect **Agitated Alba** with **Motive to kill Coachen**. If what Yew said was true, Alba might be Coachen's killer, which could also be the reason he was trying to stop your investigation. Coachen could have been the one to betray Alba by hiring a thief to steal the real Primidux Statue, so the ambassador killed Coachen as a result. Now you must find out how he did it.

Examine the **photo** near the flower wreath. It shows the Steel Samurai with the two ambassadors before they presented him with the bouquets. **Examine Alba's bouquet**. You haven't seen the yellow flower in the picture before, but you feels like it resembles something you have seen. Highlight the **yellow flower** and **deduce** with the **Allebahstian Knife** that the handle of the knife blends in with the flowers, which could be how it was carried over to Babahl!

The **Commemorative Photo** is added to your Organizer. The knife in the photo and the knife you have are both missing one petal, meaning that it's the same knife!

The **Allebahstian Knife** is updated in your Organizer.

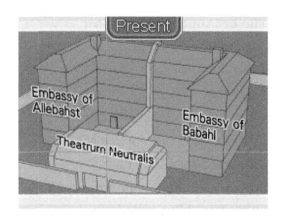

You conclude that Alba was afraid that we will find out where Coachen was really killed. This has to be a place where the Allebahstian ambassador and the Babahlese secretariat can be at the same time. **Present** the **Theathrum Neutralis**. It's the only place he could've done the deed, and if it did happen here, it would remove one of his extraterritorial rights of committing a crime on Allebahstian soil!

Your next move would be to check out the immigration records of both countries. Franziska is already one step ahead of you, though, having obtained the security footage from both embassies. The **Security Footage** is added to your Organizer.

You check Allebahst's footage first. There was no one there during 5:21 PM, Ambassador Alba walked through there

during 5:22 PM and the Steel Samurai followed at 5:23 PM. Choose to investigate the **5:23 PM** footage, and **examine** the **cart**. You note the odd shape of the bulge underneath the doll, but you won't be able to find out anything unless you have the real thing to inspect. The **Pushcart** is added to your Organizer.

Next, you inspect Babahl's footage. No one passed through there after the show, which means Coachen never returned to his embassy. With that, your investigation is complete!

Bad Ending Nine: If you fail your logic here, Alba forces you out. He says that we won't meet again but he will pray for success.

Stalling the ambassador

Ambassador Alba enters the Theatrum Neutralis. He claims that he is "overcome with regret" and is taking a plane home to Allebahst. We can't do anything about it, but Ambassador Palaeno comes to help convince him to stay a little longer. Alba only lets us ask one more question, so Edgeworth asks about his alibi during Coachen's murder.

Alba's Testimony: Ambassador Alba's Alibi

1. Frankly, I still don't understand why I am being placed under suspicion here.
2. Under your hypothetical scenario,

Mr. Coachen and I were fellow smugglers.

3. But to get to the point, I was in Allebahst the whole time.

4. So, it's simply not possible for me to have killed him in Babahl. That is my alibi.

Rebuttal: Ambassador Alba's Alibi

Press the **second statement** to get a new piece of testimony.

- In that case, what motive would I have had to kill my co-conspirator?

Present DeMasque II's Note on this statement. Coachen had planned to steal the Allebahst Primidux Statue and replace it with the old one. If he was killed, Alba could pin all the evidence and guilt of smuggling on him. Alba says that it is still a hypothesis and that he has already answered our one question. Even Palaeno's efforts to persuade him are in vain.

Kay now steps in to stall Alba from leaving. She tries to intimidate him by claiming she has evidence of the smuggling that her father obtained when he snuck into the Cohdopian embassy. Although she's simply bluffing, it is enough to force Alba to go against us one more time, but this is the very last time he'll let us do that.

Alba's Testimony: Alba's Alibi, Part 2

1. The last time I met with Mr. Coachen was here at the Theatrum Neutralis.

2. After that, I was in Allebahst the rest of the time, as I stated earlier.

3. In any case, I did not see Mr. Coachen again after that.

4. So you see, there is no time span in which I could've killed him. Wouldn't you agree?

Alba now doubles the punishment to your health bar if you press a wrong statement or present the wrong evidence. Avoid pressing **any** of the statements, or you will be striked.

Rebuttal: Alba's Alibi, Part 2

Present the **Commemorative Photo** on either the **first or fourth statement**. It shows that Alba bought the knife to the theater, meaning that he killed Coachen there. Alba doesn't care at all, as he still has extraterritorial rights even if he did murder in this neutral area. All hope seems lost...

"Not so fast!"

Agent Lang arrives just in the nick of time! He announces that Alba's diplomatic immunity has just been revoked. He had Interpol request that the imperial house of Allebahst relieves the new *Mr.* Alba of his status as an ambassador, effectively removing the second layer of his extraterritorial rights!

Alba is still not willing to surrender. He says we still don't have enough evidence to prove that he killed Coachen. The bouquet was left at the hall, so anyone could've used it to kill Coachen. He also says that we don't have a way of explaining how Coachen's body ended up in Babahl. It looks like you have a chance to make him testify again.

Alba's Testimony: Alba's Alibi, Part 3

1. I killed Mr. Coachen in this theatre using a knife that was stuck in my bouquet?
2. I left that bouquet in the theatre! Anyone could've taken the knife from there!
3. Besides, Mr. Coachen's body was discovered in Babahl, right?
4. There is no way for me to have transported his body from the theatre to Babahl!

Rebuttal: Alba's Alibi, Part 3

Present the **Pushcart** on the **fourth statement**. From the security footage, the pushcart had an unnatural bulge in it. Present the **Notes on Coachen's Body**. It was likely Coachen's body that was causing the bulge. Alba says you don't actually have the pushcart, so it is all just a theory.

"*Hold it!*"

Gumshoe suddenly arrives with the very pushcart we need! He says he found the cart at the edge of the open-air stage but didn't the Steel Samurai family only visit

Allebahst? You now inspect the cart in detail. **Examine** the **bloodstain** inside the cart. It is likely Coachen's, which proves that his body was moved using the pushcart by the Steel Samurai! Alba moved the body into Allebahst, where he could tamper with it, then smuggled it across the border and into Babahl. Let's hear what he has to say for himself.

Alba's Testimony: Movements in Allebahst

1. After I returned to Allebahst, I had my picture taken with the Steel Samurai, shaking hands.
2. Then, just as I was about to start my speech, the Yatagarasu appeared.
3. I feared for the national treasures, so I raced back to my office.

Rebuttal: Movements in Allebahst

Press every statement, but you won't find any contradiction. You still couldn't bring Alba down after all...

"*Hold it!*"

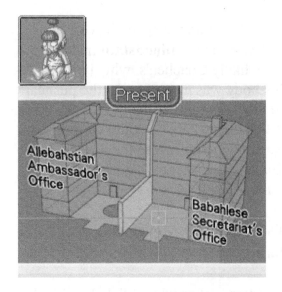

Larry and Oldbag make a timely appearance... but what can they do? Larry did find the Iron Infant doll, but it is completely wet. He says he found it in Babahl, in the middle of the pool. He lost it in the Rose Garden but found it in Babahl. It somehow managed to move across the border! You've just uncovered another smuggling route. As for how this is possible, choose **Bilateral Symmetry** when prompted. Since the embassy was built with bilateral symmetry, searching Babahl's counterpart to the Rose Garden can let us find something out! **Present** the **area near the wall** where the pool should be.

Gumshoe phones you after going to investigate the open-air stage. He reveals that there is a reservoir under the stage in Babahl! Since the infant managed to move between these two bodies of water, that means they are connected somewhere underground. Lang points out that while a doll could move between the two pools, saying that a dead body could do the same is too much of a stretch. Alba did have

104

Shih-na as an accomplice who could've helped move the body. One problem with this theory is that the pool is too deep, so if she were to attempt that, she would've drowned.

It seems that Alba has won again, but you can still figure out how the body was moved. For Shih-na to move the body over from Allebahst, she would need to get rid of all the water. There was an opportunity for this, too. **Present** the **Fires in Babahl**. The water in the reservoir was used to put out the two fires in Babahl, which could drain the reservoirs enough to let Shih-na use the connecting pipe. Alba says that the pools are very deep, though, without any ladders or footholds to help move a person up or down the pools.

But there is a way for a person to move up and down in the pools. **Present** the **Fountain Spouts**. The level of the water can be controlled using these. The fires and the fire-fighting efforts directed by Shih-na were all part of the plan to empty the pools!

Alba turned off the fountain spouts in advance, then pushed the cart with the body into the pool in the rose garden. Shih-na started the fire then stayed in the pool until the fire-fighting efforts begun, which lowered the water level in both pools to let her down to the bottom. She then pushed the cart into Babahl and waited for Alba to open the fountain spouts once more, which returned the pool to its normal level while letting Shih-na and the body float to the top. After that, she moved the body into the secretariat's office and escaped using the fireplace passage.

Alba still says you have no proof that the connecting pools were used, but you do have evidence that can prove that. **Present** the **Pick**. You found this slightly wet pick near the open-air stage, but it isn't a pick at all! **Present** the **Allebahstian Knife**. The flower on the handle of the knife lacks a petal, and the "pick" fits perfectly in that position. That proves that someone smuggled the body, along with the murder weapon, across the border using the pools!

Alba is still not convinced that you've created the perfect argument. He doesn't intend to ever surrender, so you'll have to use every piece of evidence to bring him down. This is the end of the line, and you'd better be prepared to fight to the finish!

Part 5-7 - End 3

Alba's Testimony: The Steel Samurai's Show

1. I watched from the back row. The stage was well-lit, but it was dark out in the audience.
2. I swear I was there in the audience, but it's hard to prove that, I suppose.
3. I do remember the contents of the show very well, though. Is that proof enough for you?
4. Those moving scenes were seared into this old man's heart. I'll never forget them.

Rebuttal: The Steel Samurai's Show

Press the **third statement** to get Alba to elaborate on one of the scenes.

- One of the scenes was the never-before-seen "Early Summer Rain Jab" move.

Present the **Samurai Spear** on this statement. It was needed to perform the "Early Summer Rain Jab", but since Larry bent it, the finishing move was changed to the "Steel Samurai Sushi Slash". That means that Alba did not watch the show tonight!

Alba now gives you a simple reason why he made that mistake. He needed to go to the bathroom during the show, *coincidentally* by the time the scene started. Even if it is an obvious excuse, you have absolutely no way to disprove it!

"Hold it!"

Larry interjects, saying that Alba is a true Steel Samurai fan since he knew about the "Early Summer Rain Jab" move, saying that it was decided right before the show started. The move's name was decided five minutes before the show, but as Larry's spear was already bent at the time, they had to change it. This means that Alba could only have known about the move right before the show. When asked how, choose **You saw it**. Alba saw the name of the move on the whiteboard in the backstage waiting room, which means he was there at some point during the show! Another piece of evidence is also related to the waiting room. **Present** the **Pushcart**. The pushcart was left in the waiting room until it was pushed on-stage at the end of the show, after which it was wheeled into the Allebahstian embassy. That means that the killer must've visited the waiting room sometime during the show.

Alba says he did visit the waiting room but insists that it has nothing to do with the murder. He claims that he wandered into the room while going to the bathroom, and just happened to see the name of the move. You don't have any evidence to disprove that, and Agent Lang says that his men had already thoroughly investigated that room but found nothing. Is this really the end?

"Hold it!"

Oldbag interrupts, as she wants to give you a present, which turns out to be... a box of Samurai Dogs. She said that the box had a special red dot on the fan that looked like the Japanese flag, but tasted the same as the others when she sampled it.

You recall that a pile of Samurai Dogs were piled up in the waiting room, but you know that "**Rising Sun Dogs**" don't exist. The **Samurai Dogs** had to be piled into the pushcart to move them into the embassy. As you had deduced, the killer moved the **Body in the pushcart.**

You enter Logic Mode for the last time. It's time to connect these final pieces of logic which will lead you to the truth! Connect **Samurai Dogs** with **Body in the pushcart**. The **Samurai Dogs were removed** by the killer to make room for the body in the pushcart, so a bunch of them were piled up in the waiting room.

Connect the **Rising Sun Dogs** with **Samurai Dogs were removed**. If the red substance on this box was filled in when the killer was removing the boxes to make room for the killer, you can prove that the murder did happen in the waiting room.

There is one spot on this box of Samurai Dogs you just obtained that will be the coup de grace for Mr. Alba. **Examine** the **red spot**. A rising sun package of Samurai Dogs never existed, so this red spot is actually a drop of blood. Larry had to pile up the Samurai Dogs in the pushcart so that the Iron Infant could be

106

seen by the audience when placed on the pile. The killer had to remove the Samurai Dogs in the cart to make room for the body and it was during this time that the blood made its way on to this box. All the other Samurai Dogs had been confiscated by staff members to hide evidence of the murder, but lucky for you, Ms. Oldbag managed to get to one before they did.

Although you still haven't proven that Alba killed Coachen, the blood on the box proves that the murder occurred in the waiting room. Alba says that even if the blood was Coachen's, it'll prove nothing. Even if the murder did happen in the waiting room, you have no way of proving that Alba was the killer! You've had so many moments of hope, but it looks like there really is no way to take down Quercus Alba...

"Hold it!"

A forensics technician chimes in, saying that the blood type on the box doesn't match the victim's! Alba states that it means this evidence is meaningless. It could've gotten on the box long before it reached the embassy.

It might seem like the end, but the Ace Attorney series has always been known to turn around the direst situations. What would *that* man do? As Ace Attorney fans know, turning your thinking around to look at the current situation from another angle or turn the case upside down is the key trademark of the series! If the blood did get on to the box in the dressing room, there is only one person it can belong to. **Present**

Quercus Alba's profile. If the blood was spilt in the dressing room and wasn't from Coachen, the only other person it could've come from is the killer!

Coachen probably fought back before he was killed and might have wounded Alba, possibly causing him to bleed. We can prove that Alba was bleeding around the time of the murder. **Present Amb. Alba's Wound**. While he claims that he got the wound after the show, you can disprove it with a simple test.

Alba says that his wound is a stab wound, and it isn't possible for Coachen to have carried a blade with him, especially with all the strict security. Since Alba could sneak a knife through security, Coachen must also have had some way of doing so. **Present** the **Yatagarasu's Key**. It can transform from a key into a knife, so it can easily be brought into the theater in disguise. Alba couldn't simply dispose of the key after the murder, so he cleaned the blade and placed in on Coachen's body so that when it was found in his office, it would open his private safe containing evidence of him smuggling. That's it, the finishing blow!

Alba reveals that Coachen had sought to seize control of the smuggling ring by trying to remove him from his position as an ambassador. He not only killed Coachen because of his betrayal but also to shut down the whole smuggling business. Regardless of what his motive was, he will have to face the courts, either in this country or in Allebahst. Alba finally breaks down, looking like the shrivelled, weak disguise he put up by the end.

Bad Ending Ten: If you fail this argument against Alba, he doesn't care about the truth and leaves for the airport.

What really happened

Quercus Alba was the ringleader of a large multi-national smuggling ring, mainly involved in the counterfeiting of Zheng Fa bills using Cohdopian ink. His status as an ambassador granted him extraterritorial rights that let him and his secretary, Manny Coachen, counterfeit the bills using the embassy's printing press.

Around this time, Cece Yew, a witness of the smuggling ring, was killed by Coachen under the orders of Alba to silence her, setting off the first KG-8 Incident. Coachen was deemed "Not Guilty" of the murder as decisive pieces of evidence have been stolen. Colin Devorae, the secretary of Ernest Amano, CEO of the Amano Group that was working with the smugglers, was wrongly arrested as the ringleader.

Calisto Yew, a persona of one of the members of the smuggling ring, pretended to be the victim's sister. Together with the prosecutor and detective of the case, Byrne Faraday and Tyrell Badd respectively, they formed the Great Thief Yatagarasu, a group that stole the truth behind corrupt dealings and publicized it. Mr. Faraday decided to use an inverted version of the ringleader's directives card as their symbol to warn the smuggling ring. The respective talents of all three people made them very elusive.

Calisto Yew scouted out the location of their target, Byrne Faraday infiltrated the target with his knowledge and Little Thief, while Tyrell Badd hid away evidence they left behind as the lead detective of the Yatagarasu case.

After several successful operations, Alba feared that he would be found out. He commanded "Yew" to eliminate Mr. Faraday, which she planned to do by framing him as the Yatagarasu and locking him up in jail. A miscalculation forced her to kill him and a witness herself, but she was revealed as the killer by Edgeworth. "Yew" managed to escape with the Yatagarasu's Key, but Byrne Faraday's daughter Kay preserved all of his and Yew's items.

Seven years later, Akbey Hicks, an Interpol agent tracking down the smuggling ring, was killed by Cammy Meele, another member of the ring. Yew, now posing as Shih-na, was also part of Interpol, trying to thwart another agent, Shi-Long Lang's attempts at tracking down the ringleader. She met Kay by accident and realized that she still had Byrne Faraday's Little Thief, so she planned to obtain it for the smuggling ring. Jacques Portsman, another member of the ring, was ordered to infiltrate Edgeworth's office where the KG-8 Incident files were stored to steal some incriminating evidence. Portsman failed to find anything before being discovered by his partner and killing him, but Detective Badd managed to get to it. He bumped into Edgeworth just as he was about to leave but left behind a trump card that Edgeworth could use to bring down the ringleader.

Having been informed about the Little Thief by Shih-na, Alba planned to murder Coachen, who had betrayed him, and pin the crime on Kay so that he could obtain the Little Thief for smuggling operations. He announced that the embassy had received a calling card from the Yatagarasu stating that it would infiltrate the embassy during the goodwill jubilee event and had the police department on guard duty.

That day, Ambassador Palaeno and Coachen were cleaning up Coachen's office for the event as Palaeno's office was under renovation. Coachen also requested DeMasque II to steal the Allebahstian Primidux Statue, which was the real artifact. The fake Primidux Statue, which also happened to contain the plates used for Coachen's counterfeit activities, had to be moved to the third floor from the fifth. The director for the arranged Steel Samurai show decided to name the final move as the "Early Summer Rain Jab" and wrote it down on the dressing room whiteboard. Larry bent his Samurai Spear by accident, so they were forced to scrap the name at the last minute. Larry also left the pushcart, stuffed with Samurai Dogs, in the dressing room.

Ambassador Alba began his plan. He met Manny Coachen in the dressing room backstage and killed him with a ceremonial knife snuck in with his bouquet. Before he could do that, however, Coachen fought back and stabbed him with the Yatagarasu's Key. Having killed Coachen, Alba emptied the cart of Samurai Dogs and loaded the dead body into the cart. A drip of his blood landed on one of the Samurai Dogs, right in the middle of the flag on the package. During this time, Shih-na started a fire at the fourth and fifth floors of the Babahlese embassy so that the reservoirs connecting both embassies would be emptied. She also set up piles of counterfeit bills in Coachen's office to prepare for the second fire.

After the show, the Steel Samurai pushed the cart, unknowingly along with the dead body, into Allebahst. There, Alba dumped the cart into the pool in Rose Garden. The fire-fighting efforts had drained both reservoirs which Shih-na and the cart were in. Shih-na moved the body and the murder weapon into Babahl. She waited for the pools to refill then carried the body to the office using the elevator.

Alba started preparing for his "speech" in his office. He launched a crossbow arrow to the secretariat's office along with a line of wire to the opposite side where Shih-na was waiting. They switched both Primidux Statues using the ceiling fans as pulleys. Alba fired off the second arrow to send the remainder of the wire to Babahl, where Shih-na hid it in a grandfather clock. DeMasque II ran into Ambassador Alba while trying to steal the statue and was killed with it.

The speech began. The lights, which had been elaborately set up, created a shadow that looked like the Yatagarasu, causing mass panic. At the same time, the second fire began and Kay witnessed Shih-na in a coat. Shih-na lured her into Coachen's office then accused her of being the killer. Kay was found innocent but the Yatagarasu's Key Alba put on Coachen's body helped the police to open the safe, which misled them into thinking that Coachen was the ringleader. And that's where we started from...

Epilogue

You are now in the courthouse, preparing for Quercus Alba's trial. Alba is scheduled to be in another trial in Allebahst and the prosecutor will be Franziska. All of the cases we solved were connected to the smuggling ring. Cammy Meele supported smuggling operations using her job as a flight attendant, while Jacques Portsman manipulated trials involving the ring. Ernest Amano also used the connections of the Amano Group to assist the smuggling ring.

Both Allebahst and Babahl have been reunified as Cohdopia and Ambassador Palaeno has been selected as the official ambassador of Cohdopia. Kay and Agent Lang have made it to the courthouse to see the trial, with Agent Lang having a newfound respect for you. Later, the trial ends and Quercus Alba is given the guilty verdict. Now enjoy the credits that ensue!

Later that evening, you, Gumshoe, and Kay discuss the trial. The smuggling ring has begun to dissolve and with their job done, Kay wonders what to do next, believing she should form her own three-person Yatagarasu team. She begins to leave, agreeing with you that they should work hard to create a world where the Yatagarasu isn't needed. However, she stops to take one final selfie to celebrate the moment! You reflec, admitting you have a new case to look into now - not to simply find more people guilty, but to pursue the truth and use the law for good. For that is the new creed of someone who has chosen the life of a prosecutor.

Congrats on finishing *Ace Attorney Investigations: Miles Edgeworth*! Now you can enjoy the sequel! If the next mainline title is more your thing, see Phoenix Wright: Ace Attorney - Dual Destinies! If you ever need help, remember that StrategyWiki will always be here to lend a hand!

Made in the USA
Middletown, DE
29 October 2024

63512734R00064